OXFORD PLAYSCRIPTS

Dodger

Terry Pratchett

adapted by Stephen Briggs

OXFORD

UNIVERSITY PRESS

OXFORD
UNIVERSITY PRESS

Great Clarendon Street, Oxford, OX2 6DP,
United Kingdom

Oxford University Press is a department of the University of Oxford.
It furthers the University's objective of excellence in research, scholarship,
and education by publishing worldwide. Oxford is a registered trade mark of
Oxford University Press in the UK and in certain other countries

British Library Cataloguing in Publication Data

Data available

ISBN 978 019 839349 8

9 10

Printed by CPI Group (UK) Ltd, Croydon CR0 4YY

Acknowledgements
Cover: Randall Fung/Corbis; Andrew Katz/Alamy

Illustrations by Neil Chapman.

Photos: p.4: Phillip Shepherd; p.6: Rob Wilkins; p.8: GL Archive/Alamy; Hulton-
Deutsch Collection/Corbis; traveler1116/Getty; p.9: Classic Image/Alamy; Image
Asset Management Ltd./Alamy; Antonio Abrignani/Shutterstock; 11770.bbb.4/The
British Library Board

The Publisher would like to thank Jenny Roberts for writing the Activities section.

CONTENTS

ABOUT THE ADAPTER

Stephen Briggs has been involved in amateur dramatics for more years than he'd care to remember. He has adapted more than 20 of Sir Terry Pratchett's novels for the stage (three of them, including *Dodger*, for Oxford University Press). These plays have been staged by groups all over the world – in more than 20 countries from New Zealand to Zimbabwe – including a production of his *Wyrd Sisters* at the Australian Antarctic Base.

He has also, with Terry, collaborated on a range of other publishing projects – *The Discworld Companion, Nanny Ogg's Cook Book, The Discworld Mapp, The Streets of Ankh-Morpork,* and *The Wit & Wisdom of Discworld,* plus a series of Discworld-themed diaries.

Stephen records the unabridged Discworld novels for Isis Publishing (in the UK) and for HarperCollins (in the US). He has won industry awards for two of his recordings and been nominated for two others. Stephen lives in Oxford.

WHAT THE ADAPTER SAYS

The first people *ever* to dramatize the work of Sir Terry Pratchett, in any form, were the Studio Theatre Club in Abingdon, Oxon. That was in 1991 (I know – 1991!), with *Wyrd Sisters.*

We had already staged our own adaptations of other works: Monty Python's *Life of Brian* and *The Holy Grail,* and Tom Sharpe's *Porterhouse Blue* and *Blott on the Landscape.* We were looking for something new when someone said: 'Try Terry Pratchett – you'll like him.' So I ventured into the previously uncharted territory of the 'Fantasy' section of the local bookstore ('Here Be Dragons'). I read a Terry Pratchett book; I liked it. I read all of them. I wrote to Terry and asked if we could stage *Wyrd Sisters.* He said yes.

And so it all began.

Adapting the work of a well-known, much-read and living author can be a tricky process. Scenes that work well in a novel may not work so well when being read aloud, or acted out, by real people on a stage. It can be an increasing problem to try to put over the main plot while still meeting the overriding target for amateur dramatics – completing the story in no more than about two hours.

The important thing is to decide what *is* the basic plot: Anything that doesn't contribute to that is liable to be dropped in order to keep the play flowing. Favourite scenes, even favourite characters, have on occasions had to be dumped. These are hard decisions, but the book has to work as a *play*. You can't get 400 pages of novel into two hours on stage without sacrifices.

Each play also offers a challenge to directors in working out who can double for whom in order to stage it with a smaller cast, where necessary.

Terry Pratchett's books are episodic and have a sort of 'cinematic' construction; I retained this format in *Dodger*, which I adapted specifically for the Studio Theatre Club to stage in Abingdon, and used different stage areas and levels with brisk lighting changes to keep the action flowing. Set changes slow down the action, even when they're really slick. A 30-second blackout between each scene, accompanied by rustling, crashing and muffled swearing from your stage crew means that you're in danger of losing the audience. Even *ten*-second changes, if repeated often enough, will lead to loss of interest. I've been to see many productions of my plays and the best have been those that have used bare stages or composite sets – leaving the majority of the 'scene changing' to the lighting technician. The golden rule is: If you *can* do it without scene shifting, *do* it without scene shifting. It's a concept that has served radio drama very well (everyone *knows* that radio has the best scenery). And Shakespeare managed very well without it, too. In *Antony and Cleopatra*, for instance, he has a major sea battle described by two blokes standing on a hill.

Stephen Briggs

ABOUT THE AUTHOR

Sir Terry Pratchett is one of the most popular authors writing today. He is the acclaimed creator of the Discworld series, the first title of which was *The Colour of Magic* (1983). Born in Beaconsfield, Buckinghamshire in 1948, he left school early to become a reporter on the *Bucks Free Press*, in 1965. His first book, *The Carpet People*, was published in 1971. In 1979 he left journalism to work in PR, and in 1987 left public relations to write full-time. His first Discworld novel for children, *The Amazing Maurice and his Educated Rodents*, was awarded the 2001 Carnegie Medal. Worldwide sales of his books are now more than 80 million, and they have been published in 38 languages. He was knighted for services to literature in 2009. His documentary, *Terry Pratchett: Choosing to die* (2011), has won three BAFTAs, a Grierson Award and an Emmy. *The Long War*, the second volume of his science-fiction collaboration with Stephen Baxter, was published in June 2013.

WHAT THE AUTHOR SAYS ABOUT THE NOVEL

Dodger is set broadly in the first quarter of Queen Victoria's reign; in those days life in London for the poor, and most of the people were the poor, was harsh in the extreme. Traditionally, nobody very much bothered about those in poverty, but as a decade advanced, there were those among the better off who thought that their plight should be known to everybody. One of those, of course, was Charles Dickens, but not so well known was his friend Henry Mayhew. What Dickens did surreptitiously, showing the reality of things via the medium of the novel, Henry Mayhew and his confederates did simply by facts, lots and lots of facts, piling statistics on statistics; Mayhew exposed, by degrees, the grubby underbelly of the richest and most powerful city in the world.

Readers will recognize other personages from history along the way. Disraeli was certainly real, and so was Sir Robert Peel, who founded the police force in London and became Prime

Minister (twice). Joseph Bazalgette was the leading light among the surveyors and engineers who changed the face, and most importantly the smell, of London sometime after the story of Dodger has been told. Most fantastic of all was Miss Angela Burdett-Coutts, heiress of her grandfather's fortune when she was still quite young and, at that time, the richest woman in the world.

Miss Burdett-Coutts believed in helping those who helped themselves, and so she set up the 'Ragged Schools', which helped kids and even older people to get something of an education, however poor they were. She helped people start up small businesses, and all in all was a phenomenon. She plays a major role in this narrative, and since I couldn't ask her questions, I had to make some informed guesses about the way she would react in certain circumstances. I assumed that a woman as rich as her without a husband would certainly know her own mind.

There were indeed toshers (people who searched in sewers for objects of value), whose life was anything but glamorous. But I have to admit, as Mark Twain did many years ago, that I may have put a little touch of shine on things.

I have to confess ahead of the game that certain tweaks were needed to get people in the right place at the right time – students of history will know that Sir Robert Peel was Home Secretary before Victoria came to the throne, for instance – but they are not particularly big tweaks, and besides, *Dodger* is a fantasy based on a reality. This is a historical fantasy, and certainly not a historical novel.

Although I may have tweaked the positions of people and possibly how they might have reacted in certain situations, the grime, squalor and hopelessness of an underclass which nevertheless survived, often by a means of self-help, I have not changed at all. It was also, however, a time without such things as education for all, health and safety, and most of the other rules and impediments that we take for granted today. And there was always room for the sharp and clever Dodgers, male and female.

Terry Pratchett

CHARACTER BIOGRAPHIES

Some of the characters in *Dodger* are based on real Victorian people. Some information about their lives is included here.

Henry Mayhew (1812–1887)

Henry Mayhew was a London-born author and social reformer. He was a journalist for *The Morning Chronicle*, as well as a playwright, novelist and travel writer. Mayhew's most famous work is his study of London street life, *London Labour and the London Poor* (first published in three volumes in 1851, with an additional fourth volume in 1861). The book documents the harsh realities of Victorian lower-class life and resulted in the establishment of a special Labour and the Poor Fund.

Charles Dickens (1812–1870)

Charles Dickens was a celebrated Victorian novelist. As well as authoring 15 novels and numerous short stories (including *A Christmas Carol*, *Oliver Twist* and *Great Expectations*), Dickens was also a keen journalist; in August 1834 he was appointed to the reporting staff of a leading newspaper, *The Morning Chronicle*. Dickens was a close friend of Angela Burdett-Coutts and worked with her to set up a home for homeless women, along with a number of 'Ragged Schools'.

Baroness Angela Burdett-Coutts (1814–1906)

Angela Burdett-Coutts was a Victorian philanthropist and social reformer, and a lifelong friend of Charles Dickens and Benjamin Disraeli. Burdett-Coutts became the richest woman in England when she inherited her grandfather's fortune in 1837. She used this money to fund a vast number of charitable projects, including 'Ragged Schools' for deprived children, a home for homeless women, and a scheme for improved sanitation of slum areas in London.

Sir Robert Peel (1788–1850)

Sir Robert Peel was a prominent politician and founder of the London police force. Peel twice served as Prime Minister: first from 1834–1835 and then again from 1841–1846. As Prime Minister, Peel introduced a number of important laws designed to help the poor, including the Mines and Collieries Act 1842 and the Factories Act of 1844, which limited working hours for women and children in factories.

Benjamin Disraeli (1804–1881)

Benjamin Disraeli was another prominent Victorian politician. He was a great supporter of Peel and finally became Prime Minister himself in 1868, and then again from 1874–1876. Disraeli also concentrated largely on social reform during his time in power, passing laws on public health and appropriate working conditions for factory labourers.

Sir Joseph Bazalgette (1819–1891)

Sir Joseph Bazalgette was a renowned civil engineer. In 1849, he became involved in public health engineering when he agreed to work on an ambitious project to create an improved sewer network for central London. At the time, lots of sewage ran freely through the streets of London and heavily polluted the Thames. Bazalgette was responsible for overseeing the construction of more than 1300 miles of sewers in London.

Sweeney Todd (fictional)

Sweeney Todd, often called 'The Demon Barber of Fleet Street', is a fictional London barber and murderer. The first reference to the character in literature appeared in the serialized story *The String of Pearls* (1846–1847), wherein the character murders wealthy clients for their valuables, and his neighbour uses the dead bodies to make pies. The legend is still part of popular culture, with a film adaptation directed by Tim Burton released in 2007.

A Note on Staging

This play was first performed at the Unicorn Theatre in Abingdon, by the Studio Theatre Club, on 22–26 January 2013. The dramatization was originally written with the Unicorn Theatre's restrictions, and the number of players I expected to have available, in mind. Really complicated scenic effects were virtually impossible. Basically, we had a bare stage with an onstage balcony at the back of the stage and a small curtained area beneath it. Anyone thinking of staging a Pratchett play can be as imaginative as they like – call upon the might of Industrial Light & Magic, if it's within their budget. But *Dodger can* be staged with only a relatively modest outlay on special effects. Bigger groups, with teams of experts on hand, can let their imaginations run wild!

For our staging, I used a couple of smoke machines to bring in some moody London fog, and to provide a 'miasma' in the sewer scenes. The Unicorn stage, luckily, has a trapdoor, which was a godsend when it came to emerging from, or entering, the sewers. I also made a lot of use of carefully chosen music to link scenes and, at times, to play under scenes, to help with the mood – along with sound effects (horses and carriages on cobbled streets, street traders, etc.). Because Dodger moves around London quite quickly, I also used a laptop projector and screen, and brought up slides with Victorian engravings of the locations used (such as Buckingham Palace, an alley in London, Jacob's shonky shop) to help our audiences keep up with the plot's journeys around the city.

In short, however, my experience is that it pays to work hard on getting the costumes and lighting right, and to keep the scenery to little more than, perhaps, a few changes of level enhanced by lighting effects and carefully chosen background music. We had virtually no scenery, apart from a couple of benches made especially for the play, which could also double as high desks in the newspaper office and at the Coroner's office, along with a couple of chairs that were used for Sweeney Todd's barber shop and the Mayhews' house, etc. There's room for all sorts of ideas here.

Stephen Briggs

COSTUMES AND PROPS

The period of the play is roughly about the 1840s, but Terry Pratchett has taken some liberties with historical figures to ensure the people he wanted were all around at the right time.

In general, costumes should be in the style of *Oliver Twist*: frock coats and top hats for the wealthier men; long dresses for the women; battered jackets and hats for the underclass. Dodger should progress from an 'Artful Dodger' look of grimy trousers, shirt, cap, through his pawnbroker outfit of battered top hat and 'refurbished' suit, to his immaculate frock coat, waistcoat, top hat, etc., at Angela's party.

Scene 1:   **A street in London**
Simplicity's ornate ring

Scene 2:   **The Mayhews' house**
Bench and a cup of tea
Small coins
Dickens's business card, pocketbook and pencil
Doctor's bag

Scene 3:   **The Mayhews' house, the sewers and Solomon's tenement**
Loaves of bread (or similar food prop)

Scene 4:   **Jacob's shonky shop**
Dodger's tattered new suit and hat and coins

Scene 5:   **Offices of *The Morning Chronicle* and a coffee house**
Desk spike with notes pinned on it and papers
Dickens's business card, pocketbook and pencil
Small coins
Stumpy Higgins's knife
Chairs in the coffeehouse and two cups of coffee

Scene 6:   **The Mayhews' house**
Food package

Scene 7:   **Solomon's tenement**

11

Pocket watch, Solomon's tools and sprockets
Food package

Scene 8:　　　**A room in the Germanic Embassy**
A note with Dodger's name on it

Scene 9:　　　**Sweeney Todd's barber shop**
Sign for Sweeney Todd's shop
Cut-throat razor and razor strop
Barber's chair, sheet, shaving brush and foam
Coins (from crowd)

Scene 10:　　**A street in London**
Basket of flowers and posy of roses

Scene 11:　　**Outside Parliament**
Bench
Simplicity's ornate ring

Scene 13:　　**Solomon's tenement**
Solomon's tools, watch
Bag of money
Chamber pot

Scene 14:　　**Outside Solomon's tenement**
Chamber pot
Thug's knife
Coins
Mrs Beecham's rolling pin

Scene 15:　　**Izzy's Savile Row tailors**
Tape measure, notebook and pencil for shop assistant
Dodger's new top hat and clothes
Mirror

Scene 16:　　**Angela Burdett-Coutts's house**
Glasses and plates of canapés for party
Dickens's pocketbook and pencil

Scene 18:　　**Angela Burdett-Coutts's house**

Bazalgette's business card
Dickens's pocketbook and pencil
Slip of paper from Angela

Scene 19:   **Solomon's tenement**
Bag of jewels and money
Ledgers, files and papers from the Embassy
Large box/trunk for clothes and ladies' clothing
Scruffy scrap of paper from Mary Go Round

Scene 20:   **The Coroner's office**
Old ladies' clothing and cup of tea for Dodger

Scene 21:   **Angela Burdett-Coutts's house**
Simplicity's ornate ring

Scene 22:   **A street in London**
Large, wrapped object (to look like a wrapped corpse)

Scene 23:   **Sewers**
Footman's clothing for Simplicity
Silver coin
Gold ring for Simplicity
Lanterns

Scene 24:   **Sewers**
Sweeney Todd's razor
Knife for Hans
Pistol for Outlander
Lead piping for Simplicity
Pieces of rope
Solomon's old pistol
Simplicity's new gold ring and old ornate ring
Lanterns

Scene 25:   **A bridge in London**
Letter

Scene 26:   **Buckingham Palace**
Cushion and sword

Character List

The character list offers a lot of opportunities for 'doubling' (playing more than one part). The ages given are purely for illustration, taking account of the flexible timeline acknowledged by Terry Pratchett in setting the original book.

Dodger	A tosher; in his mid-teens
Simplicity	A princess, by marriage; in her mid-teens
Charles Dickens	A writer; in his thirties
Solomon Cohen	A watchmaker; in his sixties
Benjamin Disraeli	A politician; in his late twenties
Angela Burdett-Coutts	A philanthropist; in her thirties
Sir Robert Peel	Home Secretary; in his forties
Henry Mayhew	A social researcher and writer; in his forties
Mrs Mayhew	Henry Mayhew's wife; in her forties
Joseph Bazalgette	An engineer; in his thirties
Mrs Sharples	The Mayhews' housekeeper; in her forties
Mrs Quickly	The Mayhews' cook; in her forties
Queen Victoria	Queen of England; in her early twenties
Prince Albert	Queen Victoria's Prince Consort; in his thirties
Spymaster	A politician; in his fifties
Sweeney Todd	A barber; in his late thirties
Coroner	A public official; in his forties
Prince	A Germanic noble; in his thirties

Ambassador	A Germanic official; in his fifties
Sharp Bob	A criminal lawyer; in his forties
Police Officers (five)	Police officers; in their thirties/forties
Mrs Holland	A business-woman; in her forties
Jacob	A pawnbroker; in his forties
Mary Go Round	A street trader; in her twenties
Thug	At Sol's; in his thirties
Izzy	A Savile Row tailor; in his thirties
Doctor	A GP; in his fifties
Outlander	An assassin; in her thirties
Hans	Assistant to the Outlander; in his thirties
Newspaper Clerks	At *The Morning Chronicle*; in their late teens/ early twenties
Stumpy Higgins	A robber; in his late thirties
Doorman	At *The Morning Chronicle*; in his twenties
Dirty Benjamin	A rogue; in his thirties
Mrs Beecham	A neighbour of Solomon; in her sixties
The crowd	At Sweeney Todd's; all ages

Citizens, thugs, pawnbroker's assistant, coffee house serving staff, maids, guards, flower seller, newsboy, officers at Parliament, tailor's assistant, party serving staff, palace officials and courtiers.

DODGER

SCENE 1

*A street in London. About 1840. Dark, gloomy night. People pass to and fro, conducting business, meeting, buying, selling. As the stage empties, a girl – **Simplicity** – runs on, in a panic. Two men follow, grab her, and start to beat her. A manhole cover opens and **Dodger** emerges.*

Dodger   You let that girl alone!

*He launches himself at the men, beating them soundly and they run off, pursued by him. **Simplicity** falls to the ground. A moment, then **Dodger** returns to her side. There is a short pause, and then the noise of a coach pulling away and driving off is heard – a coach with a very screechy wheel.*

Simplicity   They want to take me back, please help me…

Dodger   Please tell me your name.

Simplicity   I must not tell anybody my name, but you are most kind, sir.

Dodger	Why were those **coves**[1] beating you up, miss? Can you tell me *their* names?
Simplicity	I should not.
Dodger	Then may I hold your hand, miss, on this chilly night?

He takes her hand, and sees the ring.

Simplicity	He said he loved me… my husband. Then he let them beat me. But my mother always said that if anyone got to England, they would be free. Do not let them take me back, sir – I do not want to go.
Dodger	Miss, I ain't no sir, I'm Dodger.
Simplicity	Thank you, Dodger. You are kind…

Dickens and Mayhew enter.

Mayhew	Good heavens, Charlie, it's a girl! Come on…

Ignoring Dodger, they move to the girl's side.

Dodger	Hey you, what are you a-doing, mister? I know your sort! Coming down here, up to no good. Blimey!
Mayhew	Now see here, you. We are respectable gentlemen who, I might add, work quite hard to better the fortunes of such poor wretched girls!
Dodger	Is that what you call it, you smarmy old gits?
Dickens	Mister Mayhew and myself are decent citizens, young man. *[To Mayhew]* Your place is closest, Henry. Do you think your wife would object to receiving a needy soul for one night? I wouldn't like to see a dog out on a night such as this.
Mayhew	Do you mean *two* dogs, by any chance?
Dodger	I ain't no dog, you nobby sticks, nor ain't she! We have our

---

1.　cove – a colloquial Victorian word for a man or fellow

pride, you know. I make my own way, I does, all **kosher**[2], straight up!

Dickens My, I admire your attitude, young man. This young lady is in a bad way. Surely you can see that. My friend's house is not too far away from here, and since you have set yourself up as her champion and protector, why then, I invite you to follow us there and witness that she will have the very best of treatment that we can afford. So, my boy, what is your name?

Dodger I'm Dodger.

Dickens And you, my lad, do you *know* this young lady?

Dodger No, guv'nor, never seen her before in my life, God's truth, and I know everybody on the street. Just another runaway – happens all the time.

Dickens Am I to believe, Mister Dodger, that you, not knowing this unfortunate woman, nevertheless sprang to her defence like a true **Galahad**[3]?

Dodger I might be, I might not. And who the hell is this Galahad cove?

Dickens Galahad was a famous hero… Never mind – you just follow us, like the knight in soaking armour that you are, and you will see fair play for this damsel. Do we have an agreement? Very well.

They exit. Blackout.

● ●

SCENE 2

*The Mayhews' house. Much later. **Dodger** sat on a bench in the Mayhews' hall. **Mrs Quickly**, the cook, enters with a cup of tea and exits just as **Dickens** enters, and sits by **Dodger**.*

---

2.   kosher – Dodger uses the word here in its colloquial sense to mean that it is all above board or legitimate.

3.   Galahad – a reference to King Arthur's most noble and gallant Knight of the Round Table

Dickens	Well now, Dodger, wasn't it? I am sure you will be very happy to know that the young lady who you helped us with is safe and sleeping in a warm bed after some stitches and some **physic**[4] from the doctor. Alas, I wish I could say the same for her unborn child, which did not survive this dreadful escapade.
Dodger	Child! I didn't know.
Dickens	Indeed, I'm sure you didn't. I wonder if those gentlemen you met who were harassing her knew about the child; perhaps we shall never find out, or perhaps we shall. And therefore, sir, here for you are your two shillings – plus one more, if you were to answer a few questions for me in the hope of getting to the bottom of this.
Dodger	What sort of questions would they be, then?
Dickens	Can you read and write, Mister Dodger?
Dodger	Is this a question that gets me a shilling?
Dickens	*[Sharply]* No, it does not. But I will spring one **farthing**[5] for that little morsel and nothing more; here is the farthing, where is the answer?
Dodger	Can read 'beer', 'gin' and 'ale'. No sense in filling your head with stuff you don't need, that's what I always say.
Dickens	You are clearly an academic, Mister Dodger. Perhaps I should tell you that the young lady had, well, she had not been well used.
Dodger	Not by me! I never done nothing to hurt her, God's truth!
Dickens	Of course. I fully accept that you did nothing to harm the lady, and I have one very good reason for saying so. On her finger there is one of the biggest and most ornate gold rings I have ever seen – the sort of ring that means something – and if you were intending to do her any harm you would

---

4. **physic** – medicine or treatment
5. **farthing** – a coin of little value

have stolen it in a wink, just like you stole my pocketbook a short while ago.

Dodger   Me, sir? No, sir. Found it lying around, sir. Honestly intended to give it back to you, sir.

Dickens   I can assure you that I believe in full every word you have just uttered, Mister Dodger. Although I must confess my admiration that in the darkness you were not only able to *see* the pocketbook, but also that it belonged to me. Since you appear to care about the young lady, perhaps you could ask around or at least listen for any news about her: where she came from, her background, *anything* about her. She was badly beaten! You may find me by daylight at *The Morning Chronicle*. Here is my card if you should need it. Charles Dickens, that's me.

Dodger   Could I see the lady, sir? I ought to know what she looks like if I'm going to ask questions around and about, and let me tell you, sir, asking questions can be a dangerous way to make a living in this city.

Dickens   There is some merit in what you say. If you are to go in there, make sure your boots are clean, and those little fingers of yours, so skilled at finding other people's property in them, just make sure nothing 'falls into them'. Do not, I repeat *not*, try that in the house of Mister Henry Mayhew.

Dodger   I'm not a thief.

Dickens	What you mean, Mister Dodger, is that you're not *only* a thief. I noted the slim crowbar you have about your person – designed for opening the lids of drain covers. From which I deduce that you are a tosher – you make a living grubbing around in the sewers, looking for any coins or jewellery that may have found its way down there.
	*The **Doctor** enters with **Mrs Sharples**, the housekeeper.*
Doctor	Very bad business, sir, very nasty. I've done the best I can; they're pretty decent stitches if I say so myself. She is, in fact, a rather robust young woman underneath it all and, as it turned out, has needed to be. What she needs now is care and attention and, best of all, time – the greatest of physicians.
Dickens	And, of course, the grace of God, who is the one that charges the least… *[Pulls out some coins and pays the **Doctor**]* Naturally, Doctor, we will see that she gets good food and drink at least. Thank you for attending, and good night to you.
	*Mrs Sharples ushers the **Doctor** out and returns.*
Dodger	No offence meant, Mister Charlie, but would you mind if I watched over the lady, you know, until dawn? Not touching or nothing, but I don't know why, I think I ought to.
Mrs Sharples	I don't wanna speak out of turn, sir. I don't mind keeping an eye on another *author of the storm*[6], as it were, but I can't be responsible for the doings of this young guttersnipe, saving your honour's presence. I hope no one will blame me if he murders you all in your beds tonight. No offence meant, you understand?
Dickens	Hear that, my friend; this lady has you bang to rights. Now I must leave the stricken young lady in the care of yourself, and the care of *you* to Mrs Sharples. 'Author of the storm', indeed; I must make a note of that.

SCENE 2

DODGER

---

6. *author of the storm* – Mrs Sharples means 'orphan of the storm'.

He pulls out a small notebook and writes.

Mrs Sharples   You can trust me, sir, indeed you can. If this young **clamp**[7] gets up to any tricks, I shall have him out of here and in front of the magistrates in very short order, indeed I will.

Dickens   Now, I really must go. Business awaits! Good night, Mister Dodger!

Blackout.

● ●

SCENE 3

*The Mayhews' hallway. Next morning. There is a knock at the door; the cook – **Mrs Quickly** – crosses, answers it, and reappears carrying some loaves of bread (or similar food prop). As she re-enters, **Mrs Sharples** brings **Dodger** on from within the house. She is pulling him quite hard by his arm.*

Mrs Sharples   All right, you young **whip-a-cracker**[8], you have had your nice warm sleep in a Christian bedroom, as promised – and, as I suspect, for the first time. Now just you get out of here, and mind! I shall be watching you like a **fork**[9] until you're out of the back door, you mark my words.

Dodger   You heard Mister Charlie, missus. He is a very important man, and he gave me a mission, so I reckon I gets a bite of breakfast before bein' slung out into the cold. And I don't think Mister Charlie would be too happy if I told him about the lack of hospitality you've shown to me, Mrs Sharp Pulls.

*He rubs the arm she has been pulling him by. **Mrs Quickly** laughs.*

Mrs Quickly   OK, lad, I've got some porridge on the boil – you can have some of that, and a piece of mutton that's only slightly on the nose, and I dare say you've eaten worse. Will that do you?

---

7.   **clamp** – Mrs Sharples means 'scamp'.
8.   **whip-a-cracker** – She means 'whippersnapper'.
9.   **fork** – She means she'll be watching him like a 'hawk'.

*She nods to **Mrs Sharples**, who exits.*

That old baggage will swear blind that you must have picked up a lot of trinkets when you were here last night, and you may be sure that the real picker-up of those trinkets will have been that lady herself. And that might not look good to your new friends Mister Dickens and Mister Mayhew, right?

She gives him an appraising look.

You're a tosher, ain't you?

Dodger   Oh yes, missus.

Mrs Quickly   Right, well, let's sort you out some breakfast, yes? And remember – come and see Quickly if you ever feel the need for a friend. I mean what I say; if I can ever help you, you just have to whistle. And if I knock on your door in hard times, don't leave it shut.

*She exits. Light change. **Dodger** turns to the audience.*

Dodger   A good breakfast – and a bit of mutton to take away with me. Could be a good day today.

*He drops down into the sewer. Lights change to 'sewer' lighting. **Dodger** re-enters.*

Welcome to London's sewers. Oh, a bit of sunshine is OK – but you can't beat the shadows, the sewers, the 'solace of darkness'. There'll be other toshers down here, of course, but they don't have my nose for gold and silver. After a storm, like last night's, it mostly smells like, well, wet dead things, rotten potatoes and bad air – and, these days unfortunately, erm… well, shall we say 'excrement'? 'Cos these days toffs are getting pipes run from their **cesspits**[10] into the sewers – really unfair. 'Cos, y'know, being a tosher means that you have to feel around for all those little *heavy* things that would get caught up on the crumbling brickwork as the water went past. Best of all is the places where the

10. **cesspit** – a pit dug into the ground used for disposing waste and sewage

water swirls around in a little whirlpool capturing pennies, sixpences, farthings and – if you are very, very blessed – sometimes even sovereigns, brooches, golden rings. In the meantime, I make a living. Enough to pay my rent with old Solomon for the rooms I share with 'im.

Lights change completely to daylight. The scene has now moved to Solomon's tenement. **Solomon** *enters.*

Solomon   Charlie Dickens, you say, Dodger? I've heard of him down at the synagogue. He is a sharp cove, he is, sharp as a razor, sharp as a snake, so they tell me. So now old Solomon is thinking, why did a man like him give a job of police work to a snotty-nosed tosher like you? And it is snotty – I know you know how to use a wipe, I taught you how; just sucking it down and spitting it out on the pavement is distasteful. Are you listening? And a good start would be to *look* like someone else, especially if you are to do this work for that Mister Charlie. So while *I* am making the dinner, I want *you* to go to see my friend Jacob, down at the **shonky shop**[11]. Tell him I sent you, and that he is to dress you from head to toe with decent **schmutter**[12].

Blackout.

. . . .

SCENE 4

Jacob's shonky shop – a pawnbroker's. Later that day. **Jacob** *and an* **assistant** *enter, carrying items of clothing into which* **Dodger** *changes during the scene.*

Jacob   So – good morning Dodger! *[To his **assistant**]* My boy, this is Mister Dodger, who once heroically saved the life of my oldest friend, Solomon!

Dodger   Good morning Jacob! But I ain't a hero, I…

---

11. **shonky shop** – a shop selling second-hand goods, often with an undesirable reputation
12. **schmutter** – clothes

| Jacob | Just because we are not one of the nobby shops you find in Savile Row and Hanover Square, does not mean we have to sacrifice on customer service, eh? Although quite probably in those places the clothes you put on haven't already been worn by four or five people before you. |

Jacob and the assistant bustle around, saying things like 'Try these, oh dear no!' or 'How about this? Certain to fit, oh no, never mind, plenty more for a hero!' as they dress Dodger.

| Dodger | And I wasn't a hero, Jacob, not really. I'd just been having a really bad afternoon on the tosh, and it had started to rain. |

| Jacob | This was about two years ago now, yes? |

| Dodger | Yeah, and there was two geezers kicking somebody on the pavement. So I just waded in and laid it on with a trowel. |

| Jacob | Sounds like a hero to me, eh? And you've lived with him ever since? |

| Dodger | Yeah. Well, suits us both, dunnit? Solomon brews wonderful soups; I run errands for him – scrounging wood for his fire and, sometimes, pinching coal off the Thames barges. And if I finds jewellery down in the sewers, he gets me good prices for them – or helps me get them back to their owners when we can. |

| Jacob | Rewards? |

| Dodger | Sometimes. But there's a warm glow, right, when you can get someone their wedding ring back, say. |

By now they've dressed him in most of his new kit.

| Jacob | Well now, I do not know. Upon my word, what magicians we are, ain't we? What we have created here, my son, is a gentleman, fit for any society – if they don't mind a slight smell of **camphor**[13]. But it's that or moths, everybody knows, even Her Majesty herself. And right now I reckon, |

---

13. **camphor** – a strong smelling substance often used in the Victorian period to protect clothing from moths

my dears, that if she walked in this door she would say, 'Good afternoon, young sir, don't I know you?'

Dodger It's a bit tight.

Jacob Don't worry, it'll stretch with wear. I'll tell you what I'll do. Seeing as it's you I will throw in this excellent hat, just your size if you padded it out a bit so it ain't covering your ears, and I reckon the style will soon be all the rage again.

He steps back and examines his creation.

You know, young man, what you need now is a very good shave and then you will have to poke the ladies off with a stick! Take my advice: go to a proper barber! Take the advice of your old friend Jacob.

Dodger Thanks Jacob.

*Jacob leaves the shop and starts to cross the stage. **Mary Go Round** enters.*

Morning Mary! You bin down the pub? What's new?

Mary Double Henry stopped off just now for some grub and some brandy, seeing as how he'd just had to pull another girl out of the river. He reckoned she'd jumped off the bridge in Putney. Probably pregnant.

Dodger   Yeah. They often is. Comin' here from foreign parts, like Berkhamsted and Uxbridge, with high hopes of a better life… The city always eats 'em up and spits them out.

Mary   Almost always into the Thames.

Dodger   And it's not fair on watermen like Double Henry when the corpses come to the surface. They have to pull 'em out with a boat hook and row them down to the coroner of one of the boroughs.

Mary   It's so sad. They *all* have long hair. All the country girls have long hair and, well, they are also, you know, innocent. I was innocent once, Dodge. But it didn't do me any good. Then I found out what I was doing wrong. But I was born on the streets here, knew what to expect. Them poor little innocents never stand a chance when the first kind gentleman plies them with liquor. *[She sighs]* Gent tried to ply *me* with liquor once, but he ran out of money and I took most of what he had left when he fell asleep. Finest watch and chain I ever pinched. Still, them poor girls wasn't born round here like the likes of us, so they don't know nothing.

Dodger   Mary – perhaps you can help one of them girls. Last night, somebody was trying to kill a girl – one of them young innocents you was just talking about, I reckon – they beat her up, and I want to find out why. Have you heard anything?

Mary   Well, I was doing a bit of business in the Mall, day before the storm, and a nobby coach went past with its door open, you see, and this girl jumped out and had it away down the street as if she was on fire, right? And two coves dropped off the thing, right, and legged it after her, quick as you like, pushing people out of the way like they was not important.

Dodger   What sort of coach?

Mary   Pricey, nobby, two horses. *[Then a new thought]* Funny thing about that coach: There was a, like, squeal from one of the wheels, like a pig being killed. I heard it all down the road.

Dodger Thanks Mary – that's very helpful. Can you put the word out? I'd like to trace that coach.

He hands over a couple of coppers.

Mary Sure Dodger. *[Looking at the money]* Thanks!

She scuttles off back the way she came – to the pub.

Dodger *[Taking out Dickens's business card and reading it, slowly and laboriously]* 'Mr Charles Dickens, The Morning Chronicle, Fleet Street, London'.

Blackout.

• •

SCENE 5

Door to The Morning Chronicle *in Fleet Street. Shortly afterwards. A* **Doorman** *stands outside.* **Dodger** *approaches.*

Doorman Nothing here for the likes of you, boy, you have no business here and you can go and do your thieving somewhere else, you and your dreadful suit. Hah, looks like you've got it off a dead man!

Dodger My business is with Mister Dickens! He gave me a mission! And he gave me his card, and told me to meet him here; can you get that into your head, mister?

Doorman You might as well come in then. Don't steal anything.

Dodger *[Entering]* Thank you, sir, I will try my very best not to.

He enters the building. A couple of **Newspaper Clerks** *pass by. One carries a sheaf of papers, one carries a desk spike with some notes pinned on it.*

'Ere – what you got there?

Newspaper Clerk Don't you know anything? It just keeps our desks more tidy, that's all. In newspapers, the spike is where you put something that you have finished with or don't need any more.

Dodger   Why don't you just throw the stuff away, instead of cluttering up the place?

Newspaper Clerk   Are you stupid? Supposing it turns out later that it was important? Then all we'd have to do is find it on the spike.

*Dodger goes to exit to find **Dickens**. Behind him a masked man – **Stumpy Higgins** – enters, waving a knife.*

Stumpy Higgins   *[To the **Clerks**]* Give me your money or I'll gut yer like a clam. And nobody move!

Dodger   *[Grabbing the desk spike and moving quietly up behind **Stumpy Higgins**, whispering in his ear, so the **Clerks** won't hear – he knows him to be a man down on his luck and wants to give him a chance]* Drop the knife right now and run for it; either that or you will be breathing through three nostrils. Look, it's me, Dodger – you know Dodger. *[Aloud, for the benefit of the **Clerks**]* We will have none of this around here, you scallywag!

*He pushes **Stumpy Higgins** out of the office and into the street. Lights change.*

Blow me down if you aren't the dumbest thief I've ever met. You know, next time you come up **before the beak**[14] you will end up with the screws swinging on your ankles, you bloody idiot! When did you last eat?

Stumpy Higgins shrugs.

Look, here's sixpence. That should get you a decent bite and a space in the doss house. OK, now off you go – just keep on moving and get out of the neighbourhood. As far as they're concerned *[He indicates the **Clerks**]* I've never seen you before in my life. Look, if you're going to hold up something, the time to get grogged up is *after* the business, not before, right?

---

14. **before the beak** – before a judge in court

Stumpy Higgins runs off. Then, as Dodger turns back to the office, the Clerks enter with a Police Officer.

Police Officer	This gentleman was an accomplice, yes?
Newspaper Clerk	Well, no. In fact, to tell the truth, he threatened the villain with a spike and chased him away.
Police Officer	Oh, so this man here had a weapon as well?
Newspaper Clerk	Well, no. I mean, it's a spike; we have one on every desk.

Dickens enters from within the building.

Dickens   This young man is working for me, constable, and may I say that Mister Dodger has my full confidence. It would appear that he is a hero of epic proportions, having saved the *Chronicle* from the actions of such a terrible creature as the one that I've just heard spoken about. Now, Mister Dodger has confidential information for me, and I would like to take him over to the coffee house to hear what he has to say. So if you will, in fact, excuse the both of us…?

The people in the newspaper scene exit as Dickens and Dodger cross to a couple of chairs (the coffee house) and are given cups of coffee by a staff member. Buzz of background chatter. They sit.

Is there any point in my asking you for the truth about that little episode, or should we perhaps just let a veil of mystery fall over it? You, Mister Dodger, are very lucky, because something about that little escapade smells to me as bad as an extremely old cheese. You are lucky, Dodger, and the more you help me, the luckier you will become. What have you found out?

Dodger	One of my contacts did see the coach. And the girl.
Dickens	Could she identify any crest on the coach? Did she hear their accents?
Dodger	Mister Charlie, I know about what's on coaches and I know to recognize most lingos, but you see that in this I'm just like

you – I'm dealing with an informant who isn't bright enough to notice that sort of thing.

Dickens   You, Dodger, are smart, indeed, but you have so very little to be smart about. Although I do see that you have had the sense to get some new clothes, the best a shonky shop could provide. But on a lighter note, I expect you will like to hear that the young lady you rescued is recovering. And I believe there is some interest in all this in high places. The crest on her ring is providing an interesting line of enquiry, and my friend Sir Robert Peel is being rather discreet about all this, leading me to believe that there is a game afoot.

Dodger   Well, if nobody has reported somebody missing, it may just be that they either don't know they are missing, or hope to find the missing person before somebody else does, if you catch my meaning?

Dickens   Mister Dodger, you are a find! Who are you really, Dodger, and what is your story?

Dodger   Can I trust you?

Dickens   Strictly speaking, Dodger, the answer should be no. I am a writer and a journalist. However, I have **great expectations**[15] of you and would do nothing… *[He pauses, pulls out a notebook and makes a note]* Excuse me… *[He writes, and mutters to himself 'great expectations']* sometimes I need to jot down ideas as they occur to me. Now, please do continue.

Dodger   Well, I was brought up in an orphanage, you know. I was a foundling, never knew my mother. And there was a lot of bullies around there when I grew up. So I used to dodge about a bit, keep out of the way, as it were. And if I complained, they beat me to the ground. But after a while I got bigger, and I thought, I ain't 'aving this no more and

---

15. *great expectations* – The implication is that in describing Dodger, Dickens has come up with the phrase that he will use as the title for his novel *Great Expectations* (published in serial form in 1860 to 1861).

when I got up, I grabbed hold of a chair and I set about me.

Dickens And then?

Dodger Well, I got 'prenticed to a chimney sweep, being a skinny youth, see, and after a while I ran away, but not before coming out of the chimney into a bedroom, a swell bedroom, and coming out with a diamond ring what I nicked off the dressing table. And I tell you, sir, best move I ever made that was, 'cos the chimneys ain't no place for a growing lad, sir. The soot it gets in everywhere, sir, *everywhere*.

Dickens But how from there to toshing?

Dodger I had a little difficulty concerning a stolen goose and got chased by the **runners**[16], and so I hid out in the sewers, see? Then I found out about toshing and, well, that's it, sir, all of it, more or less.

Dickens I rather believe that you are an unusual one, my friend. Incidentally, my colleague and friend Mister Mayhew and his wife would very much like to meet you again, and may I suggest sometime tomorrow?

Dodger That's fine. But I must go, sir – Solomon will be expectin' me.

Blackout.

● ●

SCENE 6

*The Mayhews' house. The next day. Doorbell, off, then the **maid** (could be **Mrs Sharples**) ushers in **Dodger**.*

Dodger I'm here to see Mister Mayhew. I believe he is expecting me.

*The **maid** exits to fetch the **Mayhews** as **Mrs Quickly** enters.*

---

16. **runners** – a reference to the Bow Street Runners, a nickname given to London's first police force, which was originally based in Bow Street, London

Mrs Quickly	*[Noticing his 'new' clothes from Jacob]* My word, ain't you the toff and no mistake! Pray excuse me if I do not curtsey. *[She hugs him]* You are a hero of the hour, my little pumpkin. It seems that you, you little scallywag, single-handedly stopped that *Morning Chronicle* being overrun by robbers last night! Well, I thought to myself, if that is the selfsame young man I met the other day, then the only way he would stop anything being stolen would be to put his hands behind his back.
	The **Mayhews** *enter.* **Mrs Quickly** *curtsies and exits.*
Mayhew	It is a pleasure to make your acquaintance again, young man, especially in the light of your intervention yesterday evening of which Charlie has informed me. You are a most interesting young man. May I ask a… few personal questions? You see, I write things down for my job, or perhaps I should say my vocation. It is a matter of research – we hope to make the government see how terrible conditions are in this city. The government cannot fail to respond to a careful accumulation of evidence! How about you, Mister Dodger, who I believe is a tosher? Do you consider yourself rich, or poor?
Dodger	I reckon me and Sol aren't really the poor, sir. You know, we're doing a bit of this and a bit of that and we do pretty well, I think, compared to many, yes.
Mrs Mayhew	Sol being the gentleman of the Jewish persuasion with whom Charlie tells us you share lodgings?
Dodger	Oh, I don't think he needed any persuading, ma'am. I think he was born Jewish.
Mrs Mayhew	I must confess my admiration at the fact you have put yourself out for our young lady – especially as, I understand, you had never met before.
	She nods to **Mayhew** *and he exits to fetch* **Simplicity**.
Dodger	She was very scared.
Mrs Mayhew	Indeed. And you are a tosher? Why do you do the toshing?

Dodger	It's a living, madam. It's amazing what you can find down there.
Mrs Mayhew	How much do you glean from your labours as a tosher?
Dodger	Well, I reckon I might earn as much as a chimney sweep, with every now and again a little windfall. I go where I please, I ain't answerable to anybody, and every day is a sort of adventure. Of course, sometimes I find something down there that someone has lost, and it does my heart good to give it back to them.
Mayhew	*[Entering, with Simplicity]* Here is the young lady, whom I'm glad to say is making progress. *[To Simplicity]* My dear, this is Mister Dodger, the saviour of damsels in distress, as I believe you know. *[To Dodger]* She has not yet told us her name, so 'Simplicity' will suffice for a name, a good Christian name, until we know more. Unfortunately, I am led to believe that her life in recent times has not been… pleasant, although there are signs that at one time it may have been rather more… agreeable. After all, surely somebody must have cared for her to give her that wonderful ring she wears.
Dodger	Sir, if you do not object, I would very much like to talk to Simplicity alone. I have a feeling she might be capable of talking a little to me again.
Mayhew	Well, it would be unseemly to leave a young lady alone in your company.
Dodger	Yes, sir, and it's unseemly to beat a lady half to death and try to drown her, but that wasn't me, sir. So I think, sir, in the privacy of this house, you might allow the rule to be a little more…human?
Mayhew	I will leave the door open, sir. If Miss Simplicity agrees.
Simplicity	Please, sir, I would very much like to have a Christian word with my saviour.

Mayhew nods and exits with Mrs Mayhew.

Dodger	What is it that you would like to happen next?
Simplicity	I would like to say that I want to go home, but I have no home now. And I have to know who I can trust. Can I trust you, Dodger? I think I might be able to trust a man who has fought valiantly for a woman he doesn't even know.
Dodger	You know, I'm quite sure you can trust Mister and Mrs Mayhew.
Simplicity	No, I'm not sure. Mister Mayhew would prefer that you and I were not talking, Dodger. You saved me, you fought for me, and now you are going to do me harm? They are good people, but good people might think that they should deliver me to the agents of my husband because I am his wife.

*Dodger takes her hand and smiles at her. The **Mayhews** re-enter, with the **maid**, who helps **Simplicity** out.*

Dodger	Well, sir, madam, I've had a nice little chat with the girl. Perhaps if I could take her out for some fresh air?
Mrs Mayhew	Well, I am quite certain that sooner or later Simplicity must get out in the fresh air, so perhaps that could be arranged, Mister Dodger. But I am sure you will understand that it could only take place in the presence of a **chaperone**[17].
Dodger	Well, dear Mrs Mayhew, I can promise you that there will not be any hanky-panky, because I do not know what panky is and I've never had a hanky. Only a wipe.
Mrs Mayhew	You are a very forward young man, Mister Dodger.
Dodger	I certainly hope so, Mrs Mayhew, and I am sure you will agree with me that being forward is better by far than being backward. And I believe I care for Miss Simplicity. I was thinking too that we all want to find the coves what beat her up, so if I walked about with her in the town she might see or hear something that could give me a clue.

---

17. **chaperone** – someone (usually an older woman) who accompanies and supervises a young unmarried woman

Mayhew	You are commendably eloquent, Mister Dodger, but we – that is my wife and myself – feel there could be other aspects to this situation.
Dodger	Yes, sir, I fear there may be, and I rather think so does Charlie. I don't know what an eloquent is, but I do know London, sir, every dirty inch and where it's safe to go and where it's not safe to go.
Mrs Mayhew	Yes, Mister Dodger, I believe you do.

*She shakes **Dodger's** hand and goes. **Mayhew** also shakes his hand and exits, as **Mrs Quickly** enters.*

Mrs Quickly	Well, my lad, ain't you the rising star, hobnobbing with your elders and betters! Good for you! I reckon what I see in front of me now is not just another tosher but a smart young man for whom the world is an opportunity. Money is tight here these days – things are a bit worrying all-round, and of course you won't know it but we got rid of the second maid. If things get any worse, I reckon Mrs Sharples will be next, no loss, and then I suspect that it will be me, although I can't see Mrs Mayhew working in the kitchens. *[Hands him a package]* But I done you a package of leftovers – some cold potatoes and carrots, and a nice piece of pork. *[She hugs him]* When you rise up high, remember them as live lowly.

He turns to exit. Blackout.

• •

SCENE 7

*Solomon's tenement. Shortly afterwards. **Sol** is on stage, working at a pocket watch. **Dodger** enters with his package.*

Solomon	A busy day again, my friend, I hope it has proved fruitful? *[**Dodger** opens the package and shows him]* Very nice, really very nice and a fine piece of pork, I see; possibly a casserole later, I think. Well done.
Dodger	I thought you weren't allowed to eat pork.
Solomon	Strictly speaking, that may be so, but another set of rules

applies. Firstly, this is a gift from God and one should never refuse a gift given freely, and secondly, this pork appears to be quite good, better than usual, and I am an old man and I am… very hungry. Sometimes I think that the rules made centuries ago for the purpose of getting my forebears across the desert cannot easily be said to apply in this city, and in the circumstances I think that God will understand, or He is not the God I know. That is one of the good things about being Jewish. After my wife was killed in that **pogrom**[18] in Russia I came to England with only my tools, and when I saw the white cliffs of Dover, alone without my wife, I said, 'God, today I don't believe in you any more.'

Dodger   What did God say?

Solomon   *[Shrugging]* God said to me, 'I understand, Solomon, let me know when you change your mind', and I was really pleased with that, because I'd had my say and the world was better, and now I sit in a place that is rather dirty, but I am free. And I am free to eat pork, if God so wills it that pork comes my way. *[He indicates the watch he is working on]* To keep this watch working, Dodger, I am making sprockets, my boy. It is engrossing work requiring considerable coordination of hand and eye, but also in its way the work is very soothing, and that is why I look forward to making **a sprocket or two**[19]. It means I'm helping time know what it is, just as time knows what I will become.

Dodger   Sol – why did you come to England in the first place? Why here?

Solomon   Well, my dear, it seems to me that in the pinch most governments settle for shooting their people, but in England they have to ask permission first. Also, people don't much mind what you're doing as long as you're not making too

---

18. **pogrom** – the co-ordinated massacre of an ethnic group, usually used in relation to the Jews in Russia and Eastern Europe
19. **a sprocket or two** – Solomon's line echoes Fagin's song in the musical *Oliver!* (based on the Dickens novel, *Oliver Twist*), *You've Got to Pick a Pocket or Two*.

much noise. I like that in this country.

*As **Solomon** speaks, **Dodger** has become distracted by what he sees through the skylight. After a brief pause, he points to it.*

Dodger   What's that, Sol? Is it an angel?

Solomon   My experience of angels is somewhat limited, my boy, although I do believe they exist; however that particular angel, if I am not mistaken, is the planet Jupiter.

Dodger   What's that, then?

Solomon   You don't know? Jupiter is a gigantic world, much bigger than the Earth. It is only one of a number of worlds moving around the sun.

Dodger   Can we get to any of these worlds?

Solomon   Very unlikely, they are a long way off.

Dodger   As far away as Bristol, maybe?

Solomon   Alas, Dodger, it is much, much further away than Bristol. If you were better at your letters, Dodger, I might interest you with the works of Sir Isaac Newton.

Dodger   One day maybe. But for now, I need to be out on the streets again – finding out what's goin' on and who knows what.

Solomon   Not without washing your face you are not. You are almost a gentleman now, at least in very poor lighting, and you are on a mission of great importance, and so you must look your best, especially when you go and see Miss Simplicity again. Mind you don't get that suit dirty – I want to see you back here later with not one mark on it. And I suggest you go and find yourself a proper barber for a haircut and a professional shave.

Dodger   I know where there's a barber shop. I saw it when I was at the *Chronicle*. In Fleet Street.

Blackout.

A room in the Germanic Embassy. **Sharp Bob** *is on stage with the* **Prince**. *Also on stage are a couple of* **guards,** *and another man, the* **Ambassador**.

Prince   Mister Sharp Robert, I believe you told us that your men would have no difficulty in dealing with one simple girl. And yet, my friend, it would appear that she has twice escaped you, and you were only able to catch her once. This does not, I am sure you will not blame me for pointing out, appear to be a very good record, wouldn't you say?

Sharp Bob   Well, sir, we expected a girl, but that lady had a punch on her that knocked out one of my boys. And one of them's been in the ring, sir! She was fast and clever, sir, fighting like anything, and you did say that you wanted her back and on the boat in one piece. Unfortunately my boys, quite frankly, sir, also wanted to get home in one piece. I mean, the first time she took us by surprise, but that time she just ran and they got her back in and tied down in your coach. Of course, after that we were too late for the boat, which is why we were bringing her back to you. *[Small guilty pause]* Just as I told your colleague earlier, sir, everything would have been all right on the second try, but she kicked the door out and jumped off in the middle of that terrible thunderstorm.

Prince   And apparently, Mister Sharp Robert, a person called *[He checks a note]* Dodger actually wounded your two men, very nearly drowning one in a gutter. It seems to me that we should perhaps have employed him instead.

Sharp Bob   I can still be of some help, sir, bearing in mind that you already owe me quite a lot for having tracked her down in the first place. I believe you have had my bill for that for some time...

Prince   I would like to assume that you have some news about this little difficulty. I understand there was something further about this troublemaker. Do be so kind as to enlighten me, will you?

Sharp Bob	He has been asking around, sir, and being very, what you might call, methodical about it, sir.
Prince	Good heavens, man, surely you can use your own initiative, can you not?
Sharp Bob	The body asking the questions ain't just any nobody, if you get my drift; he's got *contacts* on the street, which makes things a little more difficult.
Prince	Is he working for a policeman… what you call, I believe, a **peeler**[20]?
Sharp Bob	No, sir, not for the peelers, sir. He's a bloke, sir, although he is really more of a geezer, sir, if you catch my meaning.
Prince	I do not intend to catch anything of yours, Mister Bob. What is a 'geezer'?
Sharp Bob	A geezer now, well, a geezer is somebody that everybody knows, and he knows everybody, and maybe he knows something about everyone he knows that maybe you wished he didn't know. Dodger now… well, Dodger's a tosher as well, which means he knows what's going on down in the sewers too. What I'm meaning to say, sir, is that he is a central kind of cove, you might say – makes the place a bit more interesting, if you know what I mean? And he's been seen mixing with some nobby types recently.
Prince	We do not have any interest in interesting people; they can be dangerous. However, if this Dodger is asking questions about the girl then he might either find her, or know where she is now, and so therefore I require you to make certain that he is watched at all times, do you understand? And, of course, it goes without saying that there should be no way that he can know that he is being spied on. Do I make myself clear, Mister Robert? Because I generally do. This is a very delicate matter, and we will be *extremely* disappointed

---

20. **peeler** – a police officer; the name derives from Sir Robert Peel, the founder of the London police force (the word 'bobby' also derives from Sir Robert's name)

should matters not be brought to a happy ending. I don't intend to expand here, but I'm sure you will understand what an ultimate failure ultimately entails. We want that girl, Mister Bob. We want her back.

Sharp Bob exits.

Ambassador Are you *quite* sure about this man, sir? After all, we *could* get the Outlander. I have made enquiries and he is free at the moment.

Prince No. The Outlander is sometimes very messy, dangerous; it might become... political, if it was known that we had called him in. We would prefer to avoid causing an... incident. No, the Outlander is the last resort. I have heard about what he did to the family of the Greek ambassador – it was entirely uncalled for. I won't dream of sending for the likes of him, until every other avenue has been fruitless. If this troublemaker persists in his trouble-making, or brings others into the affair... well, then, we may need to reconsider. For now, however, let us continue to use this Mister Robert Sharp. It surely can't be all that difficult, can it, for him to find a girl for us? To follow a grubby little guttersnipe? We can always get rid of him later if he becomes an... embarrassment.

Blackout.

● ●

SCENE 9

*Fleet Street. A sign appears over a doorway: 'Mister Sweeney Todd, Barber-Surgeon'. **Dodger** enters and reads the sign, slightly laboriously. He nods, and then enters the shop. **Sweeney** is in there alongside his chair. He is stropping a razor.*

Sweeney *[Morosely]* Good morning, sir! An excellent morning! What can I do for you today?

Dodger A shave and a haircut, if you don't mind...?

Sweeney Of course, sit down, sir.

*He sweeps a sheet around **Dodger**'s neck, and then he goes for the shaving foam and brush.*

Just mix up the soap.

Dodger *[Sniffing]* Is that a special soap, Mister Todd...? There's a very odd smell about it.

Sweeney No, just normal soap, sir. Probably the drains, sir. Had a hole knocked through from my privy into the sewer. Maybe it's that? *[He soaps up **Dodger**'s face]* You going to the boxing match Saturday, sir?

Dodger Er, no. No, I'm not.

Slight silence as he carries on foaming, then starts again to strop the razor.

Sweeney Would you like to hear a joke, sir? A merry jape?

Dodger Er... yes, all right.

Sweeney Which of Shakespeare's characters killed the most chickens?

Dodger I don't know, which of Shakespeare's characters did kill the most chickens?

Sweeney It was Macbeth. Because he did murder most foul.

Silence. It was probably an awful joke even in 1840.

Dodger	Are you feeling all right, Mister Todd? Your hands are shaking a little bit, Mister Todd.
Sweeney	[*Moving slightly away from the chair and looking out front*] They… they keep coming back. Yes, yes, coming back, trying to take me away with them… I remember them…
Dodger	Tell me what you see, Mister Todd; it sounds terrible. Can I help you?
Sweeney	Do you know what a cannonball can do, sir? Sometimes they bounce, very funny, ha, and then they are running along the ground, and then some lad… yes, some lad fresh from the farm sees it rolling along on the turf, and so like a bloody idiot he calls out to his mates, and he gives it a big kick, not knowing how much force there is still left in the ball. Which is quite enough to take off his leg, and not just his leg.
Dodger	What is it you are looking at, Mister Todd?
Sweeney	Barber-surgeon, that's me, the surgeon bit on the battlefield being somewhat akin to butchery, but slightly better paid… And I see them now… the broken men, the handiwork of God twisted into terrible shapes, terrible… and here they come… here they come, just as they always come, our glorious heroes, some seeing for those with no eyes, some carrying those with no legs, some screaming for them with no voice… I just tried to help, and yet still they come… they come here now, all the time… looking for me… And they say they aren't dead, but I know they are.

Dodger gently reaches out and takes the razor from Sweeney. As soon as he does, a Police Officer enters and grabs Sweeney, and a few of the crowd crush in, too. Another Police Officer makes his way into the cellar.

Police Officer 1	Well done, sir!
Dodger	[*Folding and pocketing the razor*] Can I help you gentlemen?
Police Officer 1	[*To nearest Crowd Member*] He just stood there. I mean, he just stood there, eyeball to eyeball with the man, not blinking

43

at all, just waiting for a moment to grab the wretched weapon! We didn't dare say a word, 'cos we saw Sweeney Todd was in some kind of dream, a dream in the mind of a man flourishing a dreadful weapon!

Police Officer 2   *[Re-entering from cellar]* I beg you, ladies and gentlemen, do not go down into the cellar. Oh no, 'cos if you do, you might see something that you really would not like to see. You must trust me on this – I was a soldier once. I was at **Talavera**[21] and that was bad enough. I mean, well, the stink! No wonder the neighbours had been complaining!

Dickens pushes through the crowd in the doorway.

Dickens   My name is Dickens, and I know young Dodger here to be a most excellent and trustworthy individual; he is also the hero who saved the staff of *The Morning Chronicle* just yesterday evening, and I'm sure you have all heard of that.

Crowd Member   I propose we make up a subscription for this young man of such exceptional valour! I pledge five crowns!

As people join in, Dickens takes Dodger aside. The Police Officers take Sweeney away.

Dickens   It would be in order to groan a little in response to your terrible encounter, my friend. Trust me as a journalist; you are a hero of the hour, again, and it would be a pity if an unguarded comment at this point spoiled things. Incidentally, my intrepid friend, it would interest you to know that I have been told just now that Mister Sweeney Todd used his razor to slit the throats of six gentlemen who came to him earlier this week for a haircut and a close shave. But for your almost magical response you would have been the seventh of them.

Dodger   I hardly touched 'im! I just took the razor off've 'im, that's all! Honest! It was as if he was seeing dead soldiers – dead men coming towards him, I swear it, and he was talking to

---

21. **Talavera** – a battle fought in Spain in July 1809 in the Peninsular War

them, like he was ashamed that he couldn't save them. I mean, I ain't no hero, 'cos I don't think he was a villain, sir, if you get my drift.

Dickens   Dear Mister Dodger, the truth, rather than being a simple thing, is constructed. We journalists have to distil the truth into stories that people can understand. There is almost always a different perspective... after all, my young Dodger, what exactly are you? A determined young man, plucky and brave? Or a street urchin with the luck of Beelzebub himself. And Mister Todd? Is he truly a demon – those six men in the cellar would say so! Or is he the victim as you would like to think of him? What is the truth? The truth is a fog, in which one man sees one thing and the other one sees something totally different.

Dodger   But – what? The truth is what you want to make it? That don't seem right!

Dickens   Mister Todd will either hang or they will send him to **Bedlam**[22]. If he's unlucky – for I doubt he would have the money necessary to ensure a comfortable stay there – it will be Bedlam. And now, my boy, I must head for Parliament – I have some business to enact, and some court reporting to do for the *Chronicle*.

Dodger   Well, if you will excuse me, sir, I too have another appointment!

Dickens   *You* have an *appointment*, Mister Dodger? My word, it seems to me that you are becoming a man for all seasons.

*Dodger looks as if he will ask what **Dickens** means, but waves it away.*

Dodger   I am taking Miss Simplicity for a walk!

*He runs off as **Dickens** crosses to the **crowd** who have been contributing money.*

---

22. **Bedlam** – the Hospital of St. Mary of Bethlehem in London, used as an asylum for the mentally ill

Dickens	*[Calling after him]* If you need me, I shall be at the Houses of Parliament!
	Blackout.

• •

SCENE 10

A street in London. About an hour later. **Dodger** *and* **Simplicity** *walk on, just like any couple sauntering through the park, as it were. A moment, and then* **Mrs Sharples** *enters, glaring and looking very fierce.*

Dodger	Simplicity, I'm so glad you've decided to come for this little walk with me.
	They pass a **flower seller**, *and* **Dodger** *buys some flowers that he gives to* **Simplicity**.
	Here is a present for you.
Simplicity	Oh, roses! Please, Dodger, I heard them talking. I am very grateful to Mrs and Mister Mayhew but… it is as I feared. I heard them say that they will be very pleased when I am sent back to the safety of my husband.
Dodger	Trust me, I'll see to it that you go somewhere else.
Simplicity	Oh, Dodger, I am so happy to meet you again. I burst into tears every night when I remember that storm and how you drove away those terrible men who were… so unkind, shall we say. I know I should not hate… but for them, yes! Because of them I must not use my proper name, and I dare not tell anyone it – not even you. For now, I *must* remain Simplicity, although I do not believe that I am very simple.
Mrs Sharples	I think this is quite enough, young man, and so I insist that we **rephrase**[23] our steps. Simplicity's condition is still very delicate, and you will do no service to let the cold find its way to her.

---

23. **rephrase** – She means 'retrace'.

46

Dodger	*[Pulling them to him]* Ladies, I believe there is a gentleman following us who means somebody harm. It may be Simplicity or it may be, well, me. For the love of God, and your job, I implore you now, without saying a word, to turn at the next corner and wait while I send the cove about his business.
Mrs Sharples	I have misjudged you, young man. And if the swine puts up a fight, pray kick him, good and proper.
	Simplicity and Mrs Sharples exit. Dodger conceals himself in a doorway. A moment, and then Dirty Benjamin enters. Dodger winds him and then pulls him to one side.
Dodger	Oh my word, Dirty Benjamin, as I live and wish I couldn't breathe. Down for a little stroll among the toffs, ain't you? What's your game today? 'Cos you have been following me a step for a step over the last seven corners I have travelled, and on one of them I crossed over my own steps. Funny, ain't it, that you should have the same roundabout journey in mind, you nasty, nasty little man. A spy! If you don't say something soon, so help me God, I will give you a pasting, see if I don't.
Dirty Benjamin	They is saying as you killed that barber, you know the one with all them dead bodies in his cellar, yeah?
Dodger	Something like that, but not all that. Now, if you are my friend you will tell me why you were following me, because if you don't I will make cold meat of you.
	Mrs Sharples re-enters with Simplicity. Mrs Sharples calls across to Dodger.
Mrs Sharples	I am sorry to interrupt your little **concussion**[24], gentlemen, but I think it is time for us to go home, if it's all the same with you?
Dodger	Benjamin, I have no beef with you. This is your last chance.

---

24. concussion – She means 'discussion'.

Tell me who you are working for and why, and I will never let on it's you. *[He whispers to him]* I have in my hand the razor of Sweeney Todd the barber, and at the moment I haven't opened the blade. But it calls to me; it calls to me to use it... So now, Benjamin, I strongly suggest you tell me who you are working for. *Do you understand?*

Dirty Benjamin It was Sharp Bob from Hackney Marshes, but the word is there's important coves wanting to know where you are, and if you've got some girl with you. That's all I know, honest to God. There's some kind of reward out.

Dodger Well, Benjamin, as a friend, I rely on you not to tell Sharp Bob that you have seen me. *[Dirty Benjamin nods]* Oh – and there was one other thing... *[He knees Dirty Benjamin violently]* Sorry, but Mrs Sharples asked me to. *[He crosses to the two ladies]* Simplicity, and you too, Mrs Sharples, listen. I have reason to fear that there are people who are searching for Simplicity to do her harm and therefore I am going to remove her from the kind embrace of the Mayhew household. It makes me shiver, it does, to think of you opening the door to them very nasty coves.

Mrs Sharples But she is in their care, Mister Dodger.

Simplicity I am a married woman whose husband turns out to be a weak and stupid boy, Mrs Sharples, and I believe that Dodger is right in this instance. So I suggest we make our way back to the house as soon as possible.

Mrs Sharples What are you going to do about him?

Dodger *[Crossing to Dirty Benjamin]* Listen, my friend, I know who you are, and I know where you live! Trust me that what you are going to do as soon as you are fit to stand is start walking up the road there, and you will go on walking as fast as you can in that direction as long as possible and you will not, repeat *not*, turn round to look behind you until it's absolutely dark, understand? Because you know me and I am Dodger. The Dodger what has Sweeney Todd's razor now! And if you do the wrong thing by me, I'll come up through the floor one night with it and make certain you never wake up.

Dirty Benjamin   I ain't never clapped eyes on you, mister, and by God I wish I ha'n't. You'll have no trouble from me.

Dirty Benjamin runs off, as we hear a Newsboy calling "Orrible murder! Read all about it! Valiant hero to the rescue!"

Dodger   And so... when we get back, if you will be so kind, help Miss Simplicity with such packing as she has, help us find a **growler**[25] and I will take her forthwith to Charlie, where we will be safe enough to discuss the next move.

Mrs Sharples   I feel I must object...

Simplicity   Mrs Sharples, I will go with Dodger. The choice or blame is mine, and I would not like to think that any harm came to the Mayhews' household because of me.

Mrs Sharples   Right-oh! *[To Dodger]* Is it true that you throttled the Demon Barber of Fleet Street with his own necktie?

Dodger   Look, he was just a very sick man, right? He thought he was killing dead men who were coming back to haunt him, right? I just took the razor off him and the peelers took him away.

Mrs Sharples   I think you are only saying that because you are modest, sir, I am sure.

Dodger   *[With a small sigh]* As you wish... but we must get you both back, and then I need to speak to the Mayhews – and then Simplicity and I need to see Mister Dickens at the Houses of Parliament.

Mrs Sharples   *[She shakes Dodger by the hand]* Well done, sir, very well done! Come on then!

They exit as the lights black out.

---

25. **growler** – a four-wheeled horse-drawn vehicle for public hire

SCENE 11

> *Outside Parliament. About two hours later. Two uniformed Officers stand at a door as **Dodger** and **Simplicity** enter.*

Dodger I am Mister Dodger and I am here to see Mister Charlie Dickens on a very important matter.

> *One of the **Officers** leaves to fetch **Dickens** as **Disraeli** enters behind **Dodger** and **Simplicity**.*

Disraeli Is this the hero, *twice* the hero of Fleet Street according to the newspapers?

> *Dickens enters.*

Dickens *[To **Simplicity**]* You are surely not the young lady I last saw fair beaten up three nights ago? *[To **Dodger**]* You can speak freely to me in front of my good friend Mister Disraeli. How are you, by the way? I am very glad to see that our young lady is progressing slowly but surely, which is very good news.

Disraeli Excuse me, but who exactly is the young lady? Would someone please introduce me?

Dickens Miss... Simplicity, may I introduce Mister Benjamin Disraeli. Ben, Miss Simplicity is the lady who has been discussed.

Simplicity What has been discussed about me, pray?

Dickens The facts of the matter are that you lived out of the country with your mother – an English teacher, working abroad. Following her sad demise, sometime in the recent past you went through a form of marriage with a prince from one of the Germanys. A short time later, you, miss, fled the country and landed up here in England – where your mother was born.

Simplicity *[Crossing the stage and sitting on a bench]* Yes. And I left, gentlemen, because my husband became, as soon as we were married, a snivelling wretch of a man. He even tried to put the blame for our so-called marriage on to me.

Dickens	*[Crossing and sitting next to **Simplicity**]* Subsequently, we have learned that two farm workers who were witness to the marriage have been found dead, and the priest who conducted the ceremony apparently lost his footing one day while inspecting the roof of his church and plunged to his death.
Simplicity	That would be Father Jacob, a decent man, and I would say not a man who easily falls off roofs. The witnesses were Heinrich and Gerta. I was told about them by the maid who brought my meals. I suspect that what you are going to try to tell me now is that my husband wants his wife back. This *[She holds up her ring]* is now the only evidence of the marriage. I believe, sir, that what you are trying to tell me is that my husband, that is to say his father, wants to see this ring back, come what may.
Disraeli	Yes, madam, so we understand.
Simplicity	*[Standing and moving to **Dodger**]* But you see, sir, there is more evidence of the marriage. That, sir, is myself. But I will not go back there because I know full well that I could simply vanish. How difficult would it be for me to disappear along with the other evidence? I know that my father-in-law got very angry when he found that his son and heir had married a girl who was not even fit to be a lady-in-waiting, let alone a princess.
Dodger	A *princess*? Blimey! Don't you have to be a knight or something even to rescue one?
Simplicity	I believe, sir, that there are those who wish me harm in this country. They have twice tried to abduct me since my arrival in England and it is only thanks to Dodger that I am here today and not on some boat back to my husband. My mother, who – yes – was English, said that in England everybody is free. I am at a loss, gentlemen – safe nowhere. Not even in England.
Dickens	*[Standing]* What do you think about this, Ben?
Disraeli	If Miss Simplicity should suffer harm while in our country,

it might not bode well for… affairs between the two governments. Right now the government of which we speak is demanding the return of this lady who is, after all, married and therefore the rightful property of her husband. There are indeed people, even here, who think it quite sensible to send her back for the sake of peace between nations. *[Dodger opens his mouth to speak but Disraeli holds up a hand]* Mister Dodger, be aware that we have had enough of wars lately – I believe you know this rather well after your run-in with our Mister Todd – and all too many of them started over trivial things and I am sure you can see why this matter is so difficult.

Dodger There is nothing complicated, sir, not one thing! A lady what has been beaten up by her old man and doesn't want any more of it ain't going back to where she is going to get more of the same!

Dickens Ben, surely it is possible for you to delay a decision on this for a little time, give us all the opportunity to consider the best next move. But there is a matter that clearly does need to be resolved right now. That is to say where this lady – a *princess* – will lay her head in the certainty that she will have one when she wakes up. You and I know the one person we could call on in these circumstances.

Disraeli You are, of course, talking about Angela?

Dickens But of course. *[To Dodger]* We have a useful friend, Miss Angela Burdett-Coutts, who I am sure will be delighted to offer shelter, faithful guards and lodging to Miss Simplicity. I, for my part, am absolutely sure that she will rise to the occasion, because I believe that she is a woman who never, ever has to care what politicians think, or kings for that matter.

Dodger How do I know I can trust you, Charlie – even if we can trust this mysterious Burdett-Coutts lady?

Simplicity I must trust *you*, Dodger. Maybe it's time for a little bit of trust on your behalf.

Blackout.

SCENE 12

Angela Burdett-Coutts's house. It is about thirty minutes later.
Angela is onstage. The maid shows in Dodger, Dickens and
Simplicity.

Angela   My dear, you must be Simplicity, and I am very pleased
to meet you. *[To Dodger]* Ah yes, the Hero of Fleet Street.
Charlie has told me about your exploits at the *Chronicle*, and
everyone is talking about your bravery this morning, and
you must believe me, I do have a notion as to what is going
on – people can be so talkative. From what my servants tell
me, Mister Dodger the hero is a very rich man. I understand
that the editor of the *Chronicle* has a total of 50 sovereigns
and what you might now call small change, with the promise
of more to come. All donated by grateful Londoners.

Angela speaks to Simplicity (possibly describing the room she
will occupy), as Dodger and Dickens move slightly apart and
speak in lowered voices.

Dodger   *[To Dickens]* But I ain't no hero, Charlie.

Dickens   Do be careful about protesting; you know who and what you
are and I suppose so do I. But right now the good people
of London have contributed this money to someone they
consider to be a hero. Who are we to deprive them of their
hero?

Dodger   And poor old Todd is a villain, right?

Dickens   Well, now – some people might think that a hero is just the
sort of man who *would* protest that the so-called villain is
nothing more than a sad, mad man in torment because of
what war has done to him, and suggest that Bedlam would
be a better option than the gallows. People might then
believe that hero, especially if he were to contribute some
of his newfound wealth seeing to it that the poor man had a
reasonable time there...?

Dodger   No one's going to listen to *me*!

Dickens   You undersell yourself, my friend. And you undersell the power of the press.

Angela   *[Crossing back to them with **Simplicity**]* Clearly the thing to do right now is to get this young lady – young *woman* – a meal and a chance to sleep in a warm and, above all, secure bedroom. Nobody comes into this house without my permission, and any intruder who came in with intent to do harm would wish they had never been born, or perhaps if they were able to think more selectively, that *I* had never been born. Simplicity is entirely welcome or, I should say…'I am welcoming the daughter of an old friend from the country, who is staying here in safety while she learns to navigate her way in this wicked city.' I am sure that you, Mister Dodger, have all your work cut out as it is. Although I would be very grateful if you would attend me here at a musical soirée tomorrow.

Dickens   Dear Angela, would it be in order to allow this young man to come tomorrow with his friend and mentor, Solomon Cohen? An excellent and renowned maker of jewellery and watches.

Angela   Capital. I would be most happy to meet him. I believe I have heard of him. As for you, Charlie, you know you are invited anyway, and I would like to have a quiet word with you after Mister Dodger has left.

Dodger   Excuse me, miss, would you allow me to see where Miss Simplicity is going to sleep?

Angela   Why, pray?

Dodger   Well, miss, I reckon I can get through most windows in this city, and if I can then so can someone more nasty than me, if you see what I mean.

Angela   You acknowledge no master, do you, Mister Dodger?

Dodger   I don't know what you mean, miss, but I want to know that Simplicity is safe, you see.

Angela   Well done, Mister Dodger. I will get Mavis to show you the room and the bars on the window. I too do not like intruders, and even now I'm wondering whether I shouldn't employ you or some of your contemporaries to find a hitherto undiscovered way in. But now perhaps you should call at the *Chronicle* offices on your way home? Collect your money? I must speak at length to Charlie.

Blackout.

SCENE 13

Solomon's tenement. Later that evening. **Solomon** *is onstage, working at a watch repair.* **Dodger** *enters, carrying a bag of money.*

Solomon   Oh, Dodger, a little late. Never mind, stew is all the better for a really good simmer... and I heard all about your exploits.

Dodger   I hope you've got some room in your strongboxes! *[He empties out the money]* It's not right though – Mister Todd wasn't no monster.

Solomon   It is not your fault if people call you a hero, but it is to your credit that you recognize that if he was a monster then it was other monstrous things which made him so. In the case of the money, one might feel that this is in some way a society trying to feel better. The people at Coutts' bank are your men, I think, and therefore I suggest that you put the money with them, where it will be safe and earn interest. A very good nest egg indeed!

Dodger   Interest? What's money interested in?

Solomon   *More* money, take it from me.

Dodger   Well, I don't want people to be very interested in me!

Solomon   You see, it is like this: supposing one of these new-fangled railway gentlemen, let us call him Mister Stephenson, has a design for a wonderful new engine. Now Mister Coutts and his gentlemen might lend him the necessary cash in order to get his good idea to a state of solid reality. It's called finance.

Dodger	This sounds a bit like gambling to me. I'm glad that Simplicity is safe where she is. But she will be in danger every time she goes for a walk, and as far as I can see there ain't nobody in the government who'd help her.
Solomon	That is because the government thinks mostly about all the people – they are not very good at individuals. The wishes of the husband are invariably considered more important than those of the wife.
Dodger	All I know is there are people who would be happy to hear that Simplicity was dead.
Solomon	Well then, Dodger, you have answered your own little conundrum. Let them hear that Simplicity is dead, mm…? No one hunts a dead man.
Dodger	What do you mean?
Solomon	I mean, Dodger, that you are a very resourceful young man, and I have given you something to think about. Think about people seeing what they want to see. Now I suggest an early night, because tomorrow we will be dining with very important people and I will feel ashamed if people were to say, 'Look at that overgrown street urchin, you can see that he has no manners at all.' They will say, I suspect, that he slurps when he drinks his soup, which you, Dodger, if I may say so, do a lot. If people like Mister Disraeli are going to be there, then you must be a gentleman and it would appear that I have less than one day to turn you into one. This is a matter of pride, Dodger, which I have and you must acquire. First thing in the morning we will go and see Mister Coutts to open you a bank account. *[**Dodger** raises a hand]* Do not argue with me. This isn't the sewers. When it comes to finance, I am a master. After that, my boy, I intend to introduce you to Savile Row. We haven't got much time, but my friend Izzy will see you right. I am certain that he will give a good deal to an old friend who, incidentally, carried

him to safety when the **Cossacks**[26] shot him.

Dodger   Savile Row is in the West End!

Solomon   Well done. Now – take the **chamber pot**[27] out to the cesspit
– it's full and we might just need it overnight.

Blackout.

● ●

SCENE 14

*Night exterior. Outside Solomon's tenement, about five minutes
later.* **Dodger** *enters with empty chamber pot.* **Thug** *enters and
holds a knife to* **Dodger**'s *throat.*

Thug   There is something of considerable importance that you
know the whereabouts of, Mister Dodger, and I'm hearing
that some people are scared of you on account of everybody
knowing, so they say, that you must be quite the lad to have
put down Sweeney Todd. But me? I say no, that can't be
true, can it, considering that all a cove needs to do is wait
right here and threaten you when you comes out to take the
air of a night. Well, there's none here but you and me. And
my employer, Mister Sharp Bob, will be all the happier. That
is, Mister Dodger, if you can tell me of the whereabouts of
that girl.

Dodger   I don't know you. Thought I knew everyone in all the
boroughs.

Thug   By now I reckon you've worked out you can't break my
grip and I could do very nasty things to your neck before
you do. I'm going to enjoy this after the way you came at
us in that storm. You might have 'eard tell that someone has
taken measures since then so as my associate of that night

SCENE 14

DODGER

---

26. **Cossacks** – people of Russian, Ukrainian and Siberian origin who, at the time Solomon
refers to, were a military force protecting Russia's borders
27. **chamber pot** – a bowl-shaped container with a handle used in the Victorian period as a
toilet; generally used during the night

is now no longer in the land of the living – and you're going to be joining 'im pretty sharpish, I reckon. I needs that information. Now.

Dodger   It sounds like I am in the hands of a professional, then.

Thug   I guess you could say that.

Dodger   Good.

*He throws his head back and headbutts the **Thug**, spins, punches him twice in the stomach, and then kicks him as he falls. He picks up the **Thug**'s knife.*

Good news is that in a couple of months you will hardly remember this; the bad news is, that after about two weeks you will need to get somebody to break that nose proper for you again so's you look like your old 'andsome self. Yes, mister, I am the geezer that knocked you down in the storm. The geezer who stood up to Mister Sweeney Todd, and do you know what? I have his razor. Oh my, how it does talk to me. You tell Sharp Bob to come and ask me questions himself, right! I ain't a murderer, but I am on good terms with such as is, and I'll see you in **lavender**[28] if I ever see you around here, you will float down the river without a boat, and that's the truth.

A window opens offstage.

Voice   *[Off]* Who's down there?

Dodger   *[Calling to the offstage voice, and any other neighbours who may be listening out]* Nothing to worry about, folks, it's me, Dodger, and a bloke from out of town who amazingly enough fell over my foot. *[He turns back to the **Thug**]* You are a very lucky man. And if I ever see your face around here again you will have what we might call a very close shave. Understand? I will assume that was a yes.

*He rifles through the **Thug**'s pockets and pulls out some coins.*

---

28. **lavender** – a reference to Lavender Hill Cemetery

*He turns and starts to exit. A lady – **Mrs Beecham** – in a nightdress and overcoat enters, carrying a rolling pin.*

Mrs Beecham   Who's that? I ain't got any money in the house, you know. Oh, it's you, young Dodger.

Dodger   Yes, it is me, Mrs Beecham, and I know you haven't got any money in the house, but you have now.

He drops the stolen coins into her hand, salutes and saunters off.

Mrs Beecham   God bless you, sir, I will say a prayer for you at church in the morning.

Blackout.

● ●

SCENE 15

*Izzy's Savile Row tailors. The next morning, about 11 o'clock. Bell. **Dodger** and **Solomon** enter.*

Dodger   Do I really need toffs' clothing? Mister Disraeli and his friends, well, they know what I am, don't they?

Solomon   And what are you exactly, my friend? Their inferior? Their employee? Or, I would suggest, their equal? As I recall, if you go around telling people that they are downtrodden, you tend to make two separate enemies: the people who are doing the downtreading and have no intention of stopping, and the people who are downtrodden, but nevertheless – people being who they are – don't want to know. They can get quite nasty about it.

Dodger   Am I downtrodden?

Solomon   You? Not so you would notice, my boy, and neither do you tread on anybody else, which is a happy situation to be in. I certainly believe that some, if not all of the people that you will meet later, will be considerably richer than you, but they will not think this means they are that much better than you. Money makes people rich; it is a myth to think it makes them better, or even that it makes them worse. People are what they do, and what they leave behind.

*Izzy enters, with his **assistant**.*

Izzy   Good morning, Solomon! How can I help you? *[He sees the way **Dodger** is dressed]* Oh no – I see how I can help you! Izzy will take care of everything – I have everything in hand. *[He starts to measure **Dodger**, calling measurements out to his **assistant**]* 36. Leave it all to Izzy, 28, and everything will not just be all right but also extremely acceptable in every possible way... 18... And at a price that will amaze and yet satisfy all parties – 22 – *[He measures **Dodger**'s inside leg]* 32. How does one dress, sir?

Dodger   Well, normally I'd put on yesterday's unmentionables if they ain't too bad, and then I pulls on my stockings... No! I tell a lie; most days I put on my vest and then I put on my socks. *[**Solomon** crosses and whispers to him]* How the hell should I know? I never bothered to look! Things find their own way, don't they? What kind of question is that to ask a man, anyway?

Solomon laughs.

Izzy   Your luck is holding, sir – I can do you a wonderful deal! It appears that another tailor was told to work on a frock coat and a very elegant waistcoat and trousers, but regrettably one of my associates made a laughable mistake during the measuring, which means that they will no longer fit the fine gentleman they were intended for, and so I have a little proposition for you, sir. I could do you an excellent deal, young sir, on a complete suit of garments; they are happily only a stitch away from your requirements at a very spirited discount of... 50%? *[He catches **Solomon**'s eye]* I beg your pardon, 75, *[Again catching **Solomon**'s eye]* sorry no, 80%. I will throw in two pairs of very elegant unmentionables as well?

Solomon   And a hat?

Dodger   I've got a hat from Jacob!

Solomon	That shonky thing? It looks like somebody used it as a concertina and handed it to a clown. You need a hat for a gentleman.
Dodger	But I am not a gentleman.
Solomon	You will be much closer to being one with an elegant hat for special occasions.

*Izzy brings in a top hat, which he places on **Dodger**'s head.
Dodger looks at himself in the mirror.*

Dodger	I rather think that one will do me a treat. Yep. A sharp look, sharp as a razor. I could be no end of a swell…
Solomon	…Where recently you have been no end of a smell! *[**Dodger** protests]* Well – no matter how hard you scrub, the curse of the tosher will always leave its own cheerful mark on you. *[He looks at the price]* One pound and eighteen shillings? Grossly extravagant!
Dodger	True, a lot of money for something I don't really need, but

the other day you said while you was working on one of your little machines that 'this thing needs oiling'. The day before *that* you said that your lathe had 'wanted' oil. So – surely – *want* is the same as *need*, yes?

Solomon   Are you certain you weren't born Jewish?

Dodger   No, I'm not, but thanks for the compliment. So, Sol, now that I have a much smarter suit of clothes – and a hat – for Miss Burdett-Coutts, tell me more about her. What does she *do*?

Solomon   A remarkable woman is Miss Burdett-Coutts. She is an heiress, and also a major philanthropist, which is somebody who gives their money away to the poor and needy – which I must make clear to you, young man, doesn't mean you, you being neither poor nor needy, just occasionally 'knee-deep' in sewage.

Dodger   *[Laughing to humour him]* That was a good one! Why on earth does she want to give so much money away?

Solomon   Because she feels that she should. She pays for the Ragged Schools, which give some kids at least an elementary education and funds scholarships to give brighter pupils the chance to go to university for an even better education. You, of course, must mind your manners my boy. Remember what I told you about how to eat with so much cutlery which, I have to reiterate, I would rather you did not attempt to steal.

Dodger   I'm not a thief! I can't help it if things are left lying around. Just kidding. I will be on my best behaviour and a credit to my wonderful clothes – if I'd known what it feels like to be among the **gentry**[29] I would have applied for a ticket a long time ago!

Blackout.

---

29. **gentry** – the upper class of society (although below the aristocracy)

*Angela Burdett-Coutts's house. Late afternoon that day. A party is in full swing. Guests, drinks, canapés, etc. **Disraeli**, **Dickens**, **Angela**, the **Mayhews**, **Bazalgette** and **Peel** are onstage. **Dodger** and **Solomon** enter; **Disraeli** crosses to them.*

Disraeli *[To **Solomon**]* How nice it is to see you here! *[To **Dodger**]* Oh, wonderful, the young tosher magically transformed into a gentleman! Excellent!

Dodger Yes, sir, indeed tonight I am a gentleman and tomorrow I might turn out to be a tosher again! I can be a gentleman, and I can be a tosher; can you be a tosher, Mister Disraeli?

A ripple of laughter around the room.

Disraeli My dear boy, do you think I would make a tosher? Hardly a profession I had reason to consider, I must say!

Dickens It's just scrambling in the mud to find the hidden treasure, my friend, and I might suggest it is remarkably like politics! If I was you I would take the opportunity to learn something very valuable about the world.

Disraeli Well, now I come to think of it, quite possibly an exploration of the underbelly of the city would be sensible at this time.

Dickens And indeed it would show, do you not think, that you are being very careful of public opinion in the matter of drainage in this city, which is in fact outdated, ancient and stench-filled, to say the least.

Disraeli Yes indeed, Charlie, I think you may have a point. Very well, Mister Dodger, I will indeed take an underground ramble with you in the public interest. Let me see – the day after tomorrow perhaps?

Dodger I would be quite happy to give you a little tour, sir. Not near the hospitals, of course. The breweries are pretty good; down there, even the rats smell good.

Dickens *[Catching **Angela**'s eye]* Here's a go, Angela. Ben and young Dodger here are hatching up a scheme to go down into our wretched sewers shortly. Don't you think that is a fine thing?

Angela   Are they? I certainly hope they tidy themselves up before they come back here again! *[To **Dodger**]* So nice to see you again, Mister Dodger. I see you have raised your game considerably when it comes to your clothing. Excellent! *[To **Solomon**]* Ah, the most learned Mister Cohen, I presume? I have heard so much about you. I believe the **Papal Nuncio**[30] told me a wonderful story about your perceptiveness.

*Simplicity joins them. **Angela** gives **Dodger** a knowing look and 'introduces' her.*

Mister Dodger, I believe you might be interested to meet Miss Simplicity Parish, a cousin of mine from the country.

Simplicity   My word, so you are the famous Mister Dodger. I am very happy to meet you.

Angela   Ah, there's Sir Robert Peel. I'm so glad he could come. I had been told that he had been held up on a bit of business at **Scotland Yard**[31].

She crosses to welcome him.

Dodger   *[To himself]* Sir Robert Peel? The Head Peeler? Crikey!

Simplicity   *[She and **Dodger** move slightly away from the crowd, to speak privately]* Are you all right, Dodger? I know you have had such a busy time, all because of me and I am so very grateful.

Dodger   Oh, don't worry about me, miss. How is life here?

Simplicity   Angela is very kind. Really very kind, and... how can I put this...? Very understanding.

Dodger   I asked you this once before, and now things is different but there's no change in the question: what would you like to

---

30. **Papal Nuncio** – an ambassador or diplomatic representative for the Catholic Church in Rome
31. **Scotland Yard** – the headquarters of the London police force, named after its postal address

happen next? Do you want to stay here?

Simplicity I know I am here because I am a problem, and I do not wish to be a problem. Sooner or later, problems get solved. I wonder how that might happen.

Dodger Supposing as you could go somewhere where you could be anybody you wanted to be? Not no problem to nobody. Because, you see, I think I might have a plan. It's quite a good plan, but I only got one part this evening so I'm still working on it. It might be risky and it could mean a bit of play-acting, but I think it will work.

Simplicity But, dear Dodger, would I be right in believing that the success of this plan will end up with you and me together somewhere safe?

Dodger Yes, that is the plan.

Simplicity I think that would be an excellent plan, Dodger, don't you?

Dodger You agree?

Simplicity Oh yes, indeed. You are kind, very kind. I don't know about loving; we shall see. I have had what I believed was love, but it was an untrue thing. But I have found that kindness lasts a lot longer than love, and, Dodger, where you are, the world seems to fizz. You make everything seem possible.

Dodger Of course we don't have to stay together if you don't want to.

Simplicity Dodger, this may be hard for you to understand, but sometimes you should just stop talking. *[She laughs]* You don't know anything about me, Dodger.

Angela and *Dickens* start to cross towards them again, with *Peel*.

Dodger Well, I expect that someone will let me find out some more at some time, please?

Angela *[Moving alongside Dodger]* Well now, Dodger, I wonder if you have met my very good friend Sir Robert Peel?

*As **Peel** steps forward, we now see that **Dodger**'s suit from Izzy was originally made for **Peel**. **Peel** and **Dodger** are dressed identically!*

I suspect you may have some things in common.

Peel	*[After a slow look at **Dodger**'s appearance]* Oh yes, the Hero of Fleet Street. I would very much like to have a quiet word with you.
Angela	Does it hurt? You wince when somebody calls you the Hero of Fleet Street. Charlie tells me that you are quite clear that people should know that the facts of the matter are not as they seem. You appear to be everywhere and into everything, rather like the infamous highwayman **Dick Turpin**[32]. What do you think about his ride to York on his mare Black Bess?
Dodger	I think he was too clever to ride all the way to York. No, I reckon he rushed up to some of his mates what he knew to be not all that matey and shouted out something like, 'Pray for me, my lads, for I am going to try to get to York this very night!' And o' course, you see, you can be certain that when you have a price on your head like he did, his mates would have sneaked on him to the peelers within ten minutes, by which time, I'd bet you a crown, our friend Dick would be in the West End with his moustache a different colour, walking around with two sporting ladies arm-in-arm.
Angela	Your reputation goes before you, Mister Dodger, as a young man of great courage and indeed understanding. And now, shall we move to the drawing room? Sir Robert?
Peel	If I may detain *our mutual friend*[33] for just a minute or two, Angela?

---

32. **Dick Turpin** – Angela is referring to the fact that, like Turpin, Dodger seems to be where there is trouble. He also refers to the – fictionalized – journey the highwayman took to York to establish an alibi.

33. *our mutual friend* – The implication is that Sir Robert Peel has introduced the phrase 'our mutual friend' to Dickens, who will go on to name his last completed novel *Our Mutual Friend* (published in 1865).

Angela	Oh, very well – but don't delay overlong, Bobbie.

*Peel and **Dodger** move off into the library of Angela's house as the guests exit to the dining room, **Dickens** making a note in his book.*

● ●

SCENE 17

*The library of Angela's house, immediately afterwards. **Peel** and **Dodger** enter. Embarrassed silence.*

Peel	I would very much like to know how you did that murder in the sewers this afternoon.
Dodger	What murder would this be? I never murdered nobody, never!
Peel	Well now, it's funny you should say that, because I believe you, but we have a dead body in the morgue and two men who say you put the poor fellow in there. And the funny thing is, I do not believe *them*.
Dodger	You say that you don't think I murdered anybody, but there are two people saying I done it, right? Who's the body what was murdered? And why ain't you taking their word against mine?
Peel	Frankly, my men know them and say that they wouldn't take the testimony of those two if the **Archangel Gabriel**[34] gave them a reference. But I ask myself, if this murder took place only a few hours ago, why did this allegation reach me instantly, do you think? I think that you have made enemies because, as Ben tells me, you appear to be compounding your heroic deeds by keeping a certain young woman safe while she is in our country. I salute you for that, but this situation cannot go on for ever. There has clearly been a murder. And indeed I must make certain that somebody

---

34. **Archangel Gabriel** – the 'messenger of God'; an angel of the highest order in the Christian Church

is brought to justice – despite the fact that the corpse concerned was a gentleman who was known as Sharp Bob.

Dodger reacts, recognizing Sharp Bob's name from his earlier chat with Dirty Benjamin.

Mister Dodger, I am the head of the police force which makes me a policeman, but I am also a politician. But there are indeed some of us who, while publicly toeing the government line, feel that an innocent person who has sought sanctuary in Britain should not be sent back to where she does not want to go. There must surely be a way to resolve this situation without risking a war.

Dodger	A war? Over Simplicity?
Peel	Mister Dodger, you and Miss Simplicity appear to be a reason why people are being killed. Now, like Charlie, I believe that somebody not so readily associated with the government could indeed be the very man to help us find a solution.
Dodger	Me?
Peel	You are the freest free agent that I can possibly imagine. And frankly, Mister Dodger, I will deny this if ever you repeat it publicly and you may be sure that my word will be taken against yours: one of the reasons I'm talking to you now is to tell you that whatever you may be planning you must not break the law. And now, without another word, we will both stroll back to the others as if we had just been discussing the very latest in modern sanitation, and I will find you again when I need to. And, Mister Dodger, this conversation and everything to do with it has never existed. Do you understand?
Dodger	Understand what, sir?
Peel	You are a quick learner, Mister Dodger.

They exit to the rest of the party. Blackout.

*Back to the main room of Angela's house, about an hour later. The guests emerge and start to exit the house. **Dodger** is among them. **Bazalgette** crosses to **Dodger**.*

Bazalgette　I hear that you habitually frequent the sewerage system.

Dodger　I'm no expert, sir, but since you ask, I am a tosher and I reckon I've been down every drain anybody can get down in the Square Mile, and then some. And you, sir, are...?

Bazalgette　Oh dear, how remiss of me. Bazalgette, Joseph Bazalgette; here is my card, sir. May I say that if you are thinking of a journey into the sewers I would be most pleased if I could come with you.

Dodger　I was planning an... expedition with Mister Disraeli and Mister Dickens. The day after tomorrow, I believe. Perhaps one more...?

Bazalgette　You must surely know that the first people to undertake the work of building these sewers were the Romans...

Dickens and Disraeli cross to them.

Dickens　Excuse me, Mister Bazalgette, I thought I must remind our friend about that trip into the sewers.

Dodger　Let us meet at the Lion in Seven Dials. I'll do a little walk around there early in the day to make sure there ain't going to be any problems because you never know.

Dickens　Now that's a sensible precaution, Dodger. I for one cannot wait to join this little **odyssey**[35]. How about you, Mister Bazalgette?

Bazalgette　Thank you so much for this, young man. I very much look forward to seeing you the day after tomorrow.

*He exits, with the last of the guests, as **Angela** and **Simplicity** enter.*

---

35. **odyssey** – an eventful journey or adventure; the *Odyssey*, an ancient Greek poem by Homer, charts the journey home of the Greek hero Odysseus after the fall of Troy

Dickens	Everything all right, Dodger?
Dodger	I ain't a believer, Charlie, but sometimes fate seems to play a hand in things. I decided to rescue Simplicity, you see. I mean, how could I have heard all the screaming above all the noise of the storm? But I heard it right enough. And so I have to think that I have been guided on a journey and I don't know where all the steps are, and I know the people who are my betters would like to see Simplicity shut away in some *bleak house*[36] somewhere, so as she would cause no trouble. *[Dickens writes in his book]* What you writing?
Dickens	*[To himself]* 'Bleak house'... *[To Dodger]* My apologies, Mister Dodger. My attempt at jotting a thought down had nothing to do with Miss Simplicity, I can assure you.
Angela	*[Crossing to them with Simplicity]* Changing times, Mister Dodger. A young queen on the throne and a new world of possibilities. Your world, should you choose to make it so. I know that Sir Robert has spoken to you, and I know why. There are wheels within wheels. Make certain now that you're not crushed between them. *[Handing him a slip of paper]* Something my dear friend Sir Robert just said to me makes me feel that you could find this place very interesting.
Dodger	Is this the way to one of your Ragged Schools?
Angela	Not exactly, Mister Dodger; it is where I think *you* might like to teach someone a lesson.
	Solomon crosses to them.
Solomon	Have you said all of your goodbyes and thank yous? Say goodbye to Miss Simplicity, and then you and myself must be going.
Simplicity	How very nice to see you again, my hero.

---

36. **bleak house** – The implication is that Dodger has introduced the phrase 'bleak house' to Dickens, who will go on to name one of his most famous novels *Bleak House* (first published in 1853).

Angela and *Simplicity* exit back into the house as *Dickens* leaves for the street.

Solomon   You must be careful; you are in the centre of things now, if you did but know it. Although there are agents of other powers in this country, I suspect they would think twice before doing any harm to Mister Disraeli or Mister Dickens, but I think the life of a tosher is one they would snuff out without a second thought. Incidentally, what is that piece of paper in your hand?

Dodger   Tell me what this means, Sol, 'cos I think this one is important. I think these people are the people what mean Simplicity harm.

Solomon   It's the address of an embassy.

Dodger   The one that prince is from?

Solomon   As a matter of fact I think I might be able to persuade the cab to go past the address.

Dodger   No, I'll come back home with you right now to see you get in all right, but then don't wait up.

Dodger exits.

Solomon   *[Calling after him as he struggles to catch up]* Please promise me, at least, that you won't kill anybody. *[Aside]* Well, unless they try to kill you first.

Blackout.

● ●

SCENE 19

*Solomon's tenement. The next morning. **Solomon** and **Dodger** are on; **Dodger** has put down on the table a bag of jewels and money, along with some ledgers and files.*

Solomon   Dodger, I do not know for certain what you think you were doing last night, but I think I can perceive, because as you know Solomon does himself have a certain wisdom of his own, that you thought you had a score to settle with somebody. Though you know that I do not tolerate thievery of any kind, I've had a word with God and he agrees with me that in the circumstances you might have wanted to set fire to the place.

Dodger   Actually, Sol, I did torch the stables, because that bloody coach was in there – that one with the screechy wheel that was there on the night I rescued her!

Solomon   I trust you let out all the horses.

Dodger   Of course.

Solomon   *[Sorting through the bag of gems]* And after all…what is jewellery? Just shiny rocks. And you have an excellent eye. Quite excellent. But I dare say that some of these **ciphers**[37] and code books might be of considerable interest to the government; there are things here in several languages which would do a great deal of damage in some quarters, and cause a great deal of rejoicing in others.

---

37. **ciphers** – a message written in secret or disguised writing, or in a code

Dodger	You can read them?
Solomon	I can read in most languages of Europe, with perhaps the exception of Welsh, which I find a tad difficult. One of these documents is a copy of a message about the Tsar of all the Russias who apparently has done something quite naughty with the wife of the French ambassador – oh dearie me, such goings on; I think it would be a very good idea if somebody like Sir Robert was made aware of this startling information. I will see to it that he gets them. Of course, I see no reason to mention anything to him about the jewellery. All I will ask from you, my friend, is that I am allowed to take this document concerning the Tsar, and quite possibly make some use of it one day...
Dodger	Solomon, could you do a little job of work for me, please? Could you melt out some gold from this haul and make a gold ring? With a decent ruby maybe? And possibly a sprinkling of diamonds to set them off?
Solomon	I would be delighted to do that for you, Dodger, and at my very best price. *[He laughs at **Dodger**'s expression]* Honestly, my friend, what must you think of me? You must understand that was just my little joke, and I do not make many of them.

Dodger starts to pull some ladies' clothes out of a box/trunk and to put them on.

	By any chance would you like an engraved inscription? Perhaps something relating to a young lady? We can agree the exact wording later, yes?
Dodger	Are you a mind-reader too?
Solomon	Of course!
Dodger	You know so much and you can do so much. Why then do you spend most of your time fiddling with bits of old jewellery and watches and so on down here in the slums when there are many other things you could be doing?
Solomon	I enjoy my chosen trade and receive good payment for doing something that gives me great pleasure. But I suppose the

main reason is that I can no longer run as fast as I once could, and death is, well, so final. *[He looks at* **Dodger***]* Do I take it your disguise as a batty old lady is about to make a reappearance then, Dodger?

Dodger   *[Pulling out a scruffy scrap of paper]* Well, Mary Go Round told me about a young girl they pulled out of the river. So I have to go and speak to the coroner down in Southwark. *[In his old lady voice]* About my poor lost niece…

He hobbles off, in old lady mode, as the lights blackout.

● ●

SCENE 20

The Coroner's office, Southwark. Later that day – about midday. The **Coroner** *enters with* **Dodger***/the old lady.* **Dodger** *carries a cup of tea.*

Dodger   *[In his old lady voice]* …She's a sweet girl… came up to London to try to improve herself and get a better job in the big city. I told her not to talk to any gentlemen on the street, sir, but you know how it is with young girls, sir, ever the prey of a dashing gentleman with money to spend. Oh dear me, if only she had listened. I shall always blame myself.

Coroner   There's no need I'm sure…

Dodger   I mean, the country ain't like the city, that's for God's certainty.

Coroner   And she was wearing a blue dress, you say?

Dodger   Yes, sir. A blue dress, sir, not very new, but very nice underthings, sir. Maybe this is important, sir; she had yellow hair, lovely yellow hair. Never cut it, not like the other girls who would cut it every year or so and sell it when the wigmakers' man came round. She wouldn't have none of that, sir, she was a very good girl…

Coroner   It would be improper of me to use the word 'luck' in this context, madam, but fortunately it may just be the case that your niece is even now lying in our mortuary and has been there for a few days. She was drawn to my attention when I visited there yesterday morning. Alas, all along the lower Thames this sad event happens far too often. In the case of this lovely young lady, I must say that I was beginning to despair that anyone would claim her as their own.

Dodger   Oh dear, whatever am I going to tell her mother? I mean, I said I'd look after her, but young girls these days...

Coroner   Yes, I fully understand. Do let me give you another cup of tea, my good woman, and I will take you to see the corpse in question.

*They move to a curtained-off area to the side of the room. The Coroner pulls back a curtain, revealing the **corpse** to **Dodger**. **Dodger** wails and falls on the **Coroner**.*

Dodger   I ain't rich, sir, really I ain't. I reckon it will take me some time to get the where-with-all for seeing her decent, sir. Do you reckon they will have her at Crossbones cemetery?

Coroner   That I cannot say, madam, but I hardly think that your dear niece so fresh from the country was anything like the sorts of girls who are usually buried at Crossbones... Madam, I cannot but be very moved by your plight and your determination to do the very best for the soul of this unfortunate young lady. I will guarantee you – we have no shortage of ice, after all – your young niece can remain here, not for ever, but certainly for a week or two, which I reckon should be enough for me to contact those others that may be able to help you in your plight.

Dodger   God bless you, sir, you truly are a gentleman, sir. I will turn over every stone, sir, so I will, right away, sir, thank you so much for all your kindness. I'll move heaven and Earth not to put you to any trouble, sir. Can't be said that we will let one of our own go into a pauper's grave, sir.

Coroner   No problem. It's the least I can do.

*The **Coroner** exits. A moment, and then **Mrs Holland** enters.*

Mrs Holland	Dodger! As I live and breathe! Up to your old tricks?
Dodger	*[In his normal voice]* Hello, Mrs Holland! Checking on the fate of one of your girls…?
Mrs Holland	I reckon you've been stirring things up, my little lad. And there's some people that I don't like the stink of the moment I hears about them, and one of them is a cove by the name of the Outlander – ever heard of him?
Dodger	No.
Mrs Holland	I don't know if I've ever met him, don't know what he looks like, but by all accounts he is your dyed-in-the-wool, stone-hard killing cove. I'm getting word that he's been asking questions about 'somebody called Dodger' and some girl. Don't know much about him. Some say he's a Dutchman, sometimes they say he's a Switzer, but always they say he is a killer, who comes out of the dark and goes back into the dark and gets his money and disappears. No one knows what he looks like, no one knows him as a friend and the only thing that anyone knows is that he likes the ladies. But no one can tell you what he actually looks like. I mean that: Sometimes they say that they've met him and he's tall and thin, and other times that he's a fairly short cove. From what I understand, I reckon he must be a master of disguise, and if he wants to talk to you he sends one of his ladies with a message. I quite like you, Dodger, you know that. I don't like the idea that he's turning up here.
Dodger	And no one's ever really seen him, yes?
Mrs Holland	No. Like I said, lots of people have seen him, but they never seem to see the same man. It might surprise you, my boy, that a nasty old creature like me has got some standards, and so if I was you, I'd keep my eyes open even if I was asleep. See you Dodger!

They exit separately as the lights black out.

Angela Burdett-Coutts's house. Later that evening. **Angela, Dodger, Simplicity** *and* **Solomon** *are onstage.*

Dodger …And I promise you that if Simplicity is spared, that poor girl up in the mortuary in Southwark will get a place in Lavender Hill cemetery; I will see to it, and flowers too. And she will get given a name, so that at least *I* can remember her, and that's it because the world is rather bad and extremely difficult and all you can do is the best you can. And I'm just Dodger.

Angela And what about this Outlander?

Dodger Him with all his ladies? Does that sound quite real? No. Maybe the Outlander has spun a little spell that makes him bigger and more dangerous than he is. Showmanship; and I have a show of my own to prepare.

Solomon Well, Dodger, you have told me your plan and I must say that you are very thorough. You are looking at a man who once got out of a jail by garrotting a gaoler with his bootlaces. It is something I regret now, while at the same time reminding myself that because of that act I am now here to tell you about the escapade – and frankly the man deserved it. As for your plan, it is bold, daring, and in the circumstances you describe, quite possibly something that will work.

Dodger Oh yes, I just know that it's going to work, no doubt about it.

Angela Well, Mister Dodger, much as I admire you, my first inclination was to utterly forbid you to attempt this curious and dangerous scheme. But even as I summoned up the breath to do so, I realized, having seen the looks that passed between the two of you and reminding myself that Simplicity is not a child but a married woman, that the best I can do is to thank you for allowing me into the secret. Will you tell us your thoughts, Mister Cohen?

SCENE 21

DODGER

| Solomon | It seems to me that the Outlander is unlikely to find Dodger before Dodger's plan comes to its conclusion. As a plan it seems to me it does have certain appealing aspects, because if it works it is unlikely anyone would wish to delve into the matter subsequently. And, of course, my spirits rise when I consider that this plan will take place on a battlefield absolutely familiar to my young friend, who as I am aware, knows every inch of the terrain. In the circumstances, I don't think **Wellington**[38] himself could do better with an army. |

| Angela | *[To Simplicity]* Well, my dear, you are your own woman and will have my support against any man who suggests otherwise. Pray tell me what you think of this hare-brained scheme, eh? |

| Simplicity | I trust Dodger, Miss Angela. After all, look at the things he has done for me already. |

| Dodger | Er, thank you. But now you got to give up your wedding ring. |

| Simplicity | It's a pretty ring, isn't it? I loved it when he gave it to me. And I thought I was married in the eyes of God. But the poor priest who conducted the ceremony is dead, and so are two good friends, so I think that God was never in this marriage. He was never there when I was beaten, or when I was dragged into that coach, and then there was Dodger. Angela, I trust my Dodger, completely. |

She drops the ring into his hand and kisses him. Blackout.

• •

SCENE 22

The street much later that night. About midnight. **Dodger** *moves across the stage carrying the* **corpse**. *He crosses to and opens a*

---

38. **Wellington** – The Duke of Wellington was Prime Minister (1828–30, 1834) and commander of the British forces who defeated the French army led by Napoleon at the Battle of Waterloo in 1815.

*trapdoor (manhole cover) and drops the body in, moving after it. A moment or two, during which a **Police Officer** and **Peel** enter and stand close to the trapdoor. **Dodger** re-emerges.*

Police Officer Sir Robert would like a word with you, my little lad.

*The **Police Officer** and **Dodger** cross to **Peel**.*

Peel Have you ever heard of the Outlander, my friend?

Dodger *[**Dodger** does not want **Peel** to know how much he knows about the Outlander]* No.

Peel The Outlander is an assassin. We presume that he is very much interested in the whereabouts of Miss Simplicity. I know, because it is my job to know these things, that a certain embassy was broken into two nights ago, with a great deal of documentation and jewellery stolen. Subsequently it appears that the burglar then saw fit to set fire to the coach house. It seems that even before the fire the offender appeared to have scratched across the crest of this coach the words, 'That's the way to do it!' I must assume that of course you know nothing about any of this?

Dodger Well, sir, as you know, we were at a jolly soirée that night. I went home with Solomon, who I am sure will testify should you require it.

Peel Mister Dodger, I am absolutely certain that Mister Cohen would say exactly that. And since we are on the subject, would you know anything about an elderly gentleman who called in at our front desk this morning with a little package of documents for me? These are very interesting documents, very interesting. Surely Solomon must have pointed out to you the worth of what you brought home?

Dodger What, sir? Sorry, sir. Solomon ain't mentioned to me anything about any documents and I ain't seen them.

Peel Ye-e-s. Mister Dodger, have you heard the phrase 'you are so sharp that you might cut yourself'?

Dodger Yes, sir, very careful with knives, sir, you can be sure of that.

Peel	I'm so glad to hear it. You may go now. Don't do it again, young man.
Dodger	Can't, sir, haven't done it once.

Peel and the Police Officer exit.

The Outlander? How hard would it be for him to wipe a snotty-nosed tosher off of the world? *[As he exits]* I'm Dodger! It will be very hard indeed!

Blackout.

• •

SCENE 23

In the sewers, the following day. Late morning. Lighting effects, dripping water. Echoing voices, off.

Bazalgette	*[Off]* So, Mister Dodger. This is quite an experience! How do you know where to look?

Dodger	*[As he, **Bazalgette, Disraeli, Simplicity** – dressed as a footman – and **Dickens** enter]* Sometimes you get a feeling and as it might be, you look at a bit of rotted old sewer wall and something tells you that it might *just* be worth fumbling around in the crumbling bricks. So you take a look, and glory be, there's a gold ring with two diamonds on it. That's what happened to me one time.
Bazalgette	But Charlie, I thought it was just to be you, me and Mister Disraeli…?
Dickens	A slight change of plan. Miss Burdett-Coutts wanted one of her young footmen to come down with us because she wants to encourage him to better himself. Maybe he might become an engineer like yourself, sir. Roger is a good boy, rather shy and does not talk much. *[He gives **Simplicity** a very pointed look]* If he is sensible.

Simplicity nods, discreetly.

Dodger	And now, gentlemen, welcome to this, my world. As you can see, in this light sometimes it even seems a little bit golden. It's amazing how the sun gets through. What do you think of it, Mister Disraeli?
Disraeli	Well, I cannot recommend the smell, but it is not quite as bad as I expected.
Dodger	It used to be nicer, in the old days. Not so good now people are banging holes through from their houses, but just step careful and, please, if I ask any of you to do anything, please do it with alacrity, without question. *[He points to a crack in the wall]* Now here's an interesting place that's occasionally kind to toshers. Mister Disraeli, will you now try your luck as a tosher? *[**Disraeli** reaches in and comes out with a silver coin]* Hello! Do we have some beginner's luck here? Let's see what you've got. *[**Disraeli** hands him the coin, reluctantly]* My word, sir, you have the luck of a tosher and no mistake. I see I had better not let you down here again, hey? *[He hands back the coin]* Shocking, isn't it, but there you go, sir, first time out and you've already earned a working man's daily

wage. I think we ought to be getting on because of the light, but maybe our young man here would like to try next time. Would you, Master Roger? You could make a day's wages like Mister Disraeli here!

Disraeli This is rather like a lucky dip, isn't it?

Simplicity reaches in and pulls out a gold ring – the one Dodger has had made for her. She gasps.

A gold ring? You must live like a lord, Mister Dodger. Well done, Miss Simplicity.

Dickens Ben, I cannot for the life of me understand why you confused this young man, handsome though he is, with the young lady in question. Quite possibly the vapours here must, I suspect, alongside your evident joy in your new-found profession, have just for a little while gone to your head.

Disraeli Yes, yes indeed. How silly of me.

Dodger If I was you, Master Roger, I'd put that ring in your pocket for safety right now.

Bazalgette *[To Disraeli]* These bricks are useless. They are rotten and should be taken out and put back, faced with ceramic tiles – that can be the only way forward; it would keep the water out.

Disraeli Alas, we don't have the money.

Bazalgette Then if you don't have the money, you have the stink. It surely cannot be healthy, sir.

There is a clang, off.

Dickens What was that, Dodger?

Dodger Could be anything, sir. A trick of the sewers, you might say. Gentlemen, if you don't mind there are a few things I'd like to look at down here. I will show you the nearest way out. Sometimes you get undesirables down here, well, more undesirable than what's down here already. I'll just have a little glance around and then come back. I'm sure it's nothing, but with Mister Disraeli here as well, I feel a little caution is sensible.

Disraeli Come along… Miss… young man. Frankly, I could do with a breath of fresh air.

Dodger *[As they go]* Probably nothing at all, nothing at all, but I had best check.

Pause, and then **Dodger** *exits, further into the sewer. Blackout.*

• •

SCENE 24

Another part of the sewer, moments later. **Dodger** *enters.*

Dodger Come along. Here I am, mister; maybe you want to be shown the sights.

Someone starts to approach, a muffled figure, **Hans**. *At this stage, the audience still believe this to be the* **Outlander**, *but he is just one of the Outlander's accomplices.* **Dodger** *slips into a crevice and pulls out Sweeney Todd's razor. The muffled figure, holding out a knife, creeps past* **Dodger**. **Dodger** *grabs him, floors him, throws away the knife and holds out the razor.*

If you know anything about me, then you know that pressed to your neck is Sweeney Todd's razor, wonderful smooth so it is, and who knows what it could cut off? Upon my word, I was expecting rather more of an assassin than this. Come on, speak up!

A hand – the **Outlander**'s – *appears, holding a pistol, and is followed by the rest of the* **Outlander**. **Dodger** *remains at this point with his knife at* **Hans**'s *throat.*

Outlander Good evening, Mister Dodger; if you look carefully, you will see that I am holding a pistol, quite a powerful one. You will stand where you are and I will pull the trigger if you move so much as an inch. Later I will kill your young lady friend… Oh dear, oh dear, why is it that everybody assumes that the Outlander is a man?

Dodger   Excuse me, miss, but why do you want to kill Simplicity?

*During this speech, **Simplicity** enters quietly behind the* ***Outlander,*** *holding a length of lead piping.*

Outlander   Because I will then be paid quite a considerable sum of money, young man. Surely you know that? Incidentally, I have no particular quarrel with yourself, although Hans – once he can stand up straight – almost certainly would quite like to have a brief, very brief, conversation with you. We just have to wait for the poor man to recover. It won't be long now, Mister Dodger. And what is it that you are staring at, apart of course from myself?

Dodger   Now!

*Simplicity whacks the **Outlander** on the head with the piping. **Dodger** grabs the **Outlander**'s gun and points it at **Hans,** who stays on the ground.*

Why did you come back?

*He passes some rope to **Simplicity** and they tie up **Hans** and the **Outlander** as **Simplicity** speaks.*

Simplicity   You know, I looked at the ring that I found, and on it I saw it said in tiny writing: 'To S, with love from Dodger'. So of course I had to come back. Well, you told me that the Outlander always had a good-looking lady with him, and I thought, well, a good-looking lady who went around with somebody like that assassin would be a very powerful woman. I wondered if you realized that; it would appear, my dearest Dodger, that I was right.

Dodger	*[To the muffled figure, **Hans**]* Can you understand English? *[The man nods]* Good, well then, if you are a good boy and do what we ask, you might see your home country again. *[To **Simplicity**]* Right now I need to be a friend to this poor man led astray by a wicked woman. So he will, I reckon, be very, very helpful...
Simplicity	What should we do now, Dodger?
Dodger	It's like the plan. You know the place I told you about. We call it The Cauldron, 'cos that is what it is like when there is a real storm, but at least it means it's a lot cleaner than most of the places down here. You remember all the lighter bricks? There's food up there, and a bottle of water too. And people will come running down when they hear the gunshot. *[He hands her Solomon's pistol]* This is Solomon's. Do you know how to fire one of these things if necessary?
Simplicity	Well, I have seen men shooting, with my... husband, and I think I can.
Dodger	Right! You just point the bit at the end at anyone you don't like, and that generally works. If all goes well, I think I should be able to come and find you around about midnight. Don't you worry now; the worst thing in these sewers right now is me, and I'm on your side. You will hear voices, but

just lie low and keep very quiet and you will know it's me that's coming to find you when you hear me whistle, just like we planned…

Simplicity   *[Kissing him]* Do you know, Dodger, your first plan would have worked too.

*She puts on the ring she had 'found' on the tosh, and then she exits, feeling her way along the sewer wall. **Dodger** exits and emerges with the **corpse**, dressed identically to **Simplicity**. He pulls out **Simplicity**'s German ring and puts it on to the **corpse**'s hand. He then takes the **Outlander**'s pistol and shoots the **corpse**.*

Dodger   *[To the corpse]* I'm sorry.

*There is a noise of splashing feet, and voices. **Dickens** enters with **Disraeli**, **Bazalgette** and a couple of **Police Officers**.*

Dickens   Dodger! Are you all right? Miss Simplicity…?

Dodger   *[Apparently upset at the death of 'Simplicity']* She's dead, she's really dead… But I did my best, I really did.

Dickens   Dead?

Dodger   Yes, Charlie, she was shot. There was nothing I could do. It was… the Outlander, a right proper assassin. What chance would the likes of me have against someone like that?

Dickens   Are you telling me the truth, Dodger?

Dodger   It all happened so quickly that it's all a bit of a fog. But yes, I'd say that's the truth of it all right.

Dickens   *[Suspiciously]* A fog, you say?

Dodger   Yes indeed, the kind of fog in which people see what they want to see.

Dickens   This corpse…?

Dodger   A poor girl's corpse… and I have the culprits and will bring them to justice with your help, Charlie, but Simplicity, I am afraid you will never see alive again.

Dickens	I cannot say I am pleased by what I hear, Mister Dodger, but here is a constable and we will follow your lead. *[To Disraeli]* Come along, Ben, as a pillar of Parliament, you should witness this.
Disraeli	*[At the **corpse**, doing his best to appear shocked]* Good lord. It would appear that Angela's footman is really… Miss Simplicity.
	Dickens also tries to look surprised. The Police Officers are genuinely taken aback.
Police Officer	If you don't mind me saying so, sir, what was a girl doing down here dressed as a man?
Dickens	Miss Simplicity was a girl who knew her own mind, I believe. But I beg of you all, please, for the sake of Miss Burdett-Coutts, let it never be known that the girl was dressed like this when she died.
Disraeli	I should think not. The death of a young girl is appalling, but a young girl in **breeches**[39]… whatever next?
Dickens	Well, we are all agreed that this lady, who is wearing breeches, is Miss Simplicity. But her death – what do you think, constable?
Police Officer	Well, sir, that's a bullet wound and one more at least with no doubt about it. But who done it? That's what I'd like to know.
Dodger	Ah well. For the answer to that, I must beg you gentlemen to follow me over here. If you would be so good as to keep your lanterns bright, you will see trussed up a lady who I think you will find is the Outlander.
Dickens	Surely not!
Dodger	She told me she was. And lying down there is 'exhibit B', her accomplice. Speaks German, that's all I know, but I rather

---

39. breeches – a form of short trousers usually stopping just below the knee

feel he will be very anxious to tell you everything, since I must tell you to the best of my knowledge he had no part in the death of Simplicity, and as far as I am aware hasn't committed any other crime in London. *[Aside, to the Police Officer]* Apart from trying to murder me. *[Holding up the pistol, and pretending to be upset at the 'death' of Simplicity]* This was the weapon, gentlemen, and there wasn't much I could do to stop her shooting Miss S... Miss...

Dickens *[Patting him on the shoulder]* Well, you couldn't have stopped a pistol, and that's the truth of it. But well done for catching the criminals. *[He takes Dodger slightly aside]* You know, clearly you've told us the truth, but I have seen a corpse or two in my time and this one appears to me to be possibly... not very fresh...?

Dodger Yes, sir, I think it's the 'miasmic effusions', sir. After all the sewers are full of death and decay, and that finds its way in, sir, believe me it does.

Dickens 'Miasmic effusions'. *[To Disraeli]* Hear that, Ben? What can we say? I think that all of us know that Mister Dodger would never have hurt Simplicity, and we all understand that he was very caring of her. So I hope that you will join me in sympathy for this young man, who despite the loss of his lady love has managed to bring a dreadful killer to justice. *[To the Police Officer]* What do you think, constable?

Police Officer Well, sir, so it seems, sir, but the coroner will have to be informed. Has the corpse any next of kin that you know of?

Dickens Alas, no. In fact, officer, I am aware that nobody really knows who she is, or where she came from. She was somewhat unfortunate – an orphan of the storm, you might say. A girl whom Miss Burdett-Coutts had taken under her wing out of the sheer goodness of her heart. What do you think, Ben?

Disraeli A dreadful matter indeed, Mister Dickens. All we can do is let the law take its course.

Dickens And may I add my own dismay at how our innocent little excursion came to such an unhappy end. *[To the **Police Officer**]* But I have taken note, constable, that the dead girl is wearing a fine gold ring, very ornate and with a **ducal seal**[40] on it too. I must ask you to take it as evidence. *[To all]* And now I think we should leave, although I think that some of us *[He looks pointedly at **Dodger**]* should wait here until the coroner's officer comes along. May I say, constable, you should approach him in all haste.

Police Officer   Yes indeed, Mister Dickens.

Dickens   Very good. But you do have here these killers, and if I was you I should right now make an immediate report and have the wagon here as soon as possible. I will wait with Mister Dodger and the pistol, if you don't mind, until you and your colleagues return. *[To **Bazalgette**]* Joseph, how do you feel?

Bazalgette   Honestly, Charlie, I have seen worse things.

Dickens   Then would you be so kind to see that Ben gets home safely? I think he is rather shaken by all of this; I am sure that it wasn't the happy little jaunt we were all expecting.

***Bazalgette** and **Disraeli** leave. The **Police Officers** help up **Hans** and the **Outlander** and take them away.*

Dickens   I am sure that the coroner will take the view that since the girl had no friends or relatives to speak of, except a young man who clearly loved her very much and a lady who had kindly given her shelter, then surely this was an open and shut case if ever there was one. Dodger, I think there is a game called *Find the Lady*, but I am not asking to play it. I simply wish to know that there is a lady to be found, in good health, as it might be, by a young man who can see through the fog. Incidentally, both as a journalist and as a man who writes things about things – and indeed people – that do not exist, I rather wonder, Mister Dodger, what you would have done if the Outlander had not turned up?

SCENE 24

DODGER

---

40. **ducal seal** – the emblem representing the house of a duke or dukedom

Dodger	Did I give very much away?
Dickens	Amazingly little. Am I to assume that the young lady we all saw so definitely dead did not die by your hand, if you will excuse me for being so blunt?
Dodger	Charlie, she was one of those girls that drowns herself in the river and no one cares very much. She will get a decent burial in a decent graveyard, which is more than she would have got in other circumstances. My plan – if the Outlander had not turned up, was simplicity itself, sir. Simplicity would have excused herself, being a very 'shy lad'. Alas, she would have wandered into the sewers where I would rush to find her. In the dark there would be a great noise of a scuffle and a scream as I fought valiantly, I'll have you know, as I came to blows with an unknown man who must have heard of our little excursion and may even now be still at large. Whereupon I would rush to meet yourself and the others and implore you all to help the dying Simplicity, and not least chase the dreadful assassin through the sewers. It would be a terrifying but fruitless pursuit.
Dickens	Dodger, you have excelled yourself and I salute you. Now I suggest that you go and find Miss Simplicity, who I imagine must by now be feeling a little chilly.
Dodger	Thank you, sir. And thank you very much for teaching me about the fog.
Dickens	Oh yes. The fog. Intangible though it is, it is a very powerful thing, is it not, Mister Dodger? I shall follow your career with great interest and, if not, with trepidation.

Dickens exits. Blackout.

• •

SCENE 25

A bridge in London. Daytime. Several months later. **Angela** *and* **Solomon** *enter, separately.*

Solomon	Ah, Miss Angela, thank you so much for coming.

Angela	Do you have any news?
Solomon	Indeed, I have had a letter – surprisingly well written – from Dodger, from *York [They both smile at this reference to the earlier discussion at Angela's about Dick Turpin]* where he went to grieve, because there he won't see anything that reminds him of poor dear Simplicity.
Angela	York, well, yes indeed, how very fitting for our little highwayman. Has anyone else enquired of you of Dodger's whereabouts, pray?
Solomon	Sir Robert was kind enough to send two of his constables to visit me two days ago, and they did ask about Mister Dodger's whereabouts, and so of course I had to tell them all that I knew, which is *of course* my duty as a good citizen. *[He gives her a knowing smile]*
Angela	Quite. Quite so. You may or may not be surprised, Mister Cohen, that I too have had a communication from a nameless person, giving me details of a place in London and – isn't this quite exciting? – a time as well. This is rather fun, isn't it?
Solomon	Yes, indeed. Although I must say my life has been altogether too full of this kind of fun, so I now prefer working in my old carpet slippers, where fun does not usually interrupt my concentration.
Angela	Should you meet the young Mister Dodger again, please do tell him that I have reason to believe that the authorities would indeed like to speak to him, not because he has done anything wrong, but because he has the capacity, they think, to do some things very right, and for the good of the country. When I mention the word 'authorities', I mean the highest authority.
Solomon	When you say 'highest', you mean…?
Angela	Not the Almighty, at least not as far as I know, but definitely the next best thing – a lady who could make some parts of Mister Dodger's life somewhat easier. I rather think that this

is an invitation that would not be repeated if ignored.

Solomon Really? Well, in that case I'd better get my morning dress suit from Jacob and have it cleaned.

Blackout.

SCENE 26

*Buckingham Palace. The next morning, about 11 o'clock. **Dodger** and **Simplicity**, well-dressed, enter with a **palace official**. A moment, and then **Dickens**, **Solomon** and **Angela** enter – hugs/handshakes/etc. The unnamed **Spymaster** enters with **Peel** and **Disraeli**.*

Spymaster Mister Dodger, it is apparent that you got into the well-guarded embassy of a foreign power, and roamed at will among its floors and the inner rooms without ever being challenged. How on earth were you able to do this? And may I ask if you would be prepared to repeat this singular feat another time, at some other place, should we ask you to do so?

Dodger Do you want me to be a spy, is that it?

Spymaster Young man, Her Majesty's government does not spy, it merely *takes an interest,* and since both Sir Robert and Mister Disraeli have told us that while you are a scallywag you are the right kind of scallywag, of which we may wish we had a few more, Her Majesty's government might have an interest in occasionally employing you, although, having employed you, they would of course emphatically deny ever having done so.

Dodger Oh, I understand that, sir. It's a kind of fog, isn't it? I know about fogs. You can trust me on that, sir.

Spymaster It seems to me, Mister Dodger, that no one can teach you anything about fog.

Dodger I've lived in the fog all my life, sir.

Spymaster	Well, you do not need to give me an answer now, and I suggest you talk it over with your friend Mister Dickens. May I say, Mister Dodger, that there are some slightly worrying details about what happened in the sewer that memorable day which might in other circumstances have led to more investigation, were it not for the fact that you most certainly did bring to justice the notorious Outlander – a circumstance that will show our European friends what happens to assassins who dare to come to England. I'm sure we were all upset to hear of the death of the young lady known as Simplicity, and may I say you have my condolences.
Dodger	Thank you, sir. It has not been a very pleasant time lately, which was why I took a little trip out of London so that I didn't see anything that reminded me of my girl.
	*The **Spymaster** shakes his hand and leaves with **Peel** and **Disraeli**.*
Dickens	It would appear that all sins are forgiven, my friend, but of course it's such a shame that Miss Simplicity, despite all your best efforts, is now deceased; how is she, by the way?
Dodger	Simplicity is dead, Charlie, as well you know.
	*Angela crosses to them, with **Simplicity**.*
Angela	Well now, how surprising my friend, one might be mistaken in thinking that this young lady was Simplicity herself, but alas, as we both know, the poor girl is most dreadfully deceased. When we are finished here, perhaps you would allow me to take you and your new friend to Lavender Hill cemetery where I was intending to go today, because the stonemason will by now have finished poor Simplicity's gravestone.
Dickens	What is your name, young lady?

Simplicity	Serendipity[41], sir.
Dickens	Charmed to meet you. And Dodger – I gather you have been all over London today? Visiting Mister and Mrs Mayhew – and their servants? Delivering a bottle of finest whisky to the Southwark coroner?
Dodger	Debts to be repaid, Charlie. But I must move on. Simplicity was married. But Simplicity is dead. Now I have Serendipity – somebody new, and I'll help her. But I'm someone new too, and before we marry I've got to get a job, and a good one. I shall have to save the toshing for a hobby. But I don't even know how to get proper work.
Angela	Well now, from what that gentleman just said to you, I rather suspect, young Dodger, that you may be given the opportunity to take a government-paid 'holiday' in foreign parts. Congratulations to you, young man, and to you too, Miss Serendipity.

*A uniformed **palace official** enters and stands to attention. He is followed by several **courtiers**, the **Spymaster**, **Disraeli** and **Peel**. A moment, then all bow and curtsey as **Queen Victoria** and **Prince Albert** enter. They all straighten up, except for **Solomon**, who seems to have hurt his back. **Dodger** crosses to him, puts his knee in **Solomon's** back and straightens him up. Humorous sound effect.*

Dodger	Sorry about this, Your Majesty, he gets the twinging screws when he tries that.
Queen Victoria	Mister Cohen, it is a great pleasure to meet you at last; I've heard so many stories about you. You are not in pain in any way, are you?
Solomon	Nothing damaged except my self-esteem, Your Majesty, and may I say that some of the tales they tell about me are not true.

---

41. **serendipity** – a chance set of events ending happily

Prince Albert	The King of Sweden tells a very good one.
Solomon	If it was the one about the racehorse in the lodge, Your Royal Highness, alas it was true.
Prince Albert	Nevertheless – I feel quite privileged to meet you, sir.
Queen Victoria	You, then, must be Mister Dodger? You do very well around desperate criminals, I believe. Everyone is still talking about Sweeney Todd. That must have been such a terrible day for you.
Dodger	Well, Your Majesty, there he was and there I was, and there the razor was, and that was it really. To be honest, I felt sorry for the poor man.
Queen Victoria	So I have heard. It is a disquieting thought, but it is to your credit, at least. I believe that the young lady beside you is your fiancée, is that not so? Do come here, Miss Serendipity. When do you think your wedding will be, my dear?
Simplicity	Dodger says he will have to get a new job first, Your Majesty, so we don't know yet.
Queen Victoria	Indeed. What is it you do, Mister Dodger, when you are not thwarting criminals?
Solomon	He assists with the proper running of the drainage, Your Majesty.
Prince Albert	Oh, drains, we have them here and they never seem to work properly.
Queen Victoria	Well, sir, I wish you well in whatever post you eventually take. And now…
	*She looks at the **courtiers**. One places a cushion in front of **Dodger**. Another hands the **Queen** a sword.*
	We think that bravery such as yours should be recognized.
	***Dodger** comes forward and kneels.*
	What is your full name to be, Mister Dodger?
Simplicity	If it's any help, Your Majesty, I've always thought that Jack is a very nice name.

| **Queen Victoria** | If I was you, sir, I would take the advice of your lady. As all sensible husbands do. *[Dodger bows his head]* I dub thee Sir Jack Dodger, Knight of the British Empire. Arise Sir Jack. |
| | *As he stands, **Solomon**, **Dickens**, **Peel**, **Angela**, **Disraeli** and the **Spymaster** applaud, quietly.* |

Simplicity	It makes you look taller.
Queen Victoria	Indeed it does. Good day to you, Sir Jack. We wish you well in your future endeavours.
	*She and **Prince Albert**, followed by the **courtiers** and other palace officials, exit. **Dickens**, **Solomon** and all the others exit, leaving **Simplicity** and **Dodger** alone.*
Dodger	*[To **Simplicity**]* What should I do about this job offer?
Simplicity	Well, he does want you to be a spy. You can tell that by the look on his face when he says that he doesn't. For

someone like you, Dodger, it seems to me to be the perfect occupation, although I suspect it will mean learning one or two foreign languages. But I have no doubt that you will find learning them quite easy. I myself know French and German, as well as a little Latin and Greek. Not too difficult if you put your mind to it.

Dodger   Well, I know some Greek.

Simplicity   My word, Dodger, you do lead a very interesting life, don't you?

Dodger   *[Embracing her]* My love, I think it's only just beginning.

                 Blackout.

ACTIVITIES

1. WHO'S WHO?

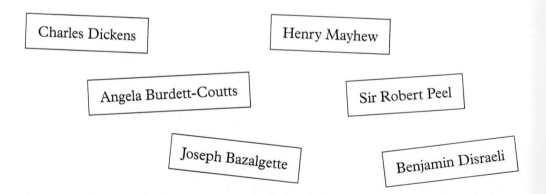

> **Objectives**
> * Understand the setting and historical context of the play.
> * Match historical people to characters in the play.

Terry Pratchett describes his novel *Dodger* as 'a fantasy based on a reality'. This means that although the story is fiction, it is rooted in a real historical setting.

In the early part of Queen Victoria's reign in the 1840s, people were flooding into the cities, in search of work and 'a better life'. Although Britain as a nation was powerful and wealthy, with an Empire that was expanding across the globe, many cities were overcrowded, smelly and dirty, and the vast majority of people were very poor. This whole underclass were largely uneducated, undernourished and struggled to survive. It was this double identity of Britain, and in particular London, that the novel and playscript *Dodger* explores.

1. Many characters in the novel are based on real people. Help to compile a short *Who's Who* by matching the correct name (below) to each description (opposite). They are all characters in the play, as well as real historical people.

Charles Dickens

Henry Mayhew

Angela Burdett-Coutts

Sir Robert Peel

Joseph Bazalgette

Benjamin Disraeli

A clever journalist who worked for *The Morning Chronicle* and later became a famous and successful novelist.

A social researcher who recorded facts about poverty in a book called *London Labour and the London Poor* (published between 1851 and 1861).

A government minister who introduced the first highly trained police force, nicknamed 'Bobbies' or 'Peelers'.

A wealthy woman who inherited a huge fortune but who spent much of her life helping to improve the lives of others. Her philanthropy included setting up schools, giving money to develop small businesses and establishing scholarships.

A clever politician (who later became Prime Minister) who recognized the need to get public opinion on his side. He helped to establish the conservative party and also wrote political novels.

Chief engineer of London's Metropolitan Board of Works and responsible for developing an efficient sewer network in the 1860s.

2. The people above were all important, successful people. Terry Pratchett explains that 'Dodger is a made-up character, as are many of the [ordinary] people he meets, although they are from types working, living and dying in London at that time.'

   Does this make the 'made-up' characters any less important than the characters based on real, successful people in this story? Talk about your views with a partner, bearing in mind that the 'made-up' characters probably represent thousands of people, rather than just individuals.

ASSESSMENT

- **Self-assessment.** Check how many characters you identified correctly by referring to your playscript.

- **Peer assessment.** Ask your partner to comment on how clearly you expressed your views about the importance of the 'made-up' characters. Ask them to choose between 'very clearly', 'fairly clearly' or 'not very clearly'.

2. THE LEGACY OF CHARLES DICKENS

> **Objectives**
>
> - Explore how *Dodger* draws on the literary heritage of Charles Dickens.
> - Compare characters and themes.

Charles Dickens was born in Portsmouth, England, in 1812. When he was only 12, his father was imprisoned for debt and Charles was forced to leave school and work in a factory to support his family. His early experience of poverty was to influence the rest of his life and work.

Eventually, Dickens became a newspaper reporter and he also began to get his fiction work published in periodicals. His novels were a huge success and he became rich and famous, travelling abroad and mixing with important people, but always expressing his concern for children's rights, education and other social reforms.

In *Dodger*, Terry Pratchett cleverly plays on the reader's knowledge about Charles Dickens and his work. As well as including 'Charlie' as a character in the story, he takes his inspiration for the main character 'Dodger' from the 'Artful Dodger' (Jack Dawkins) in *Oliver Twist*.

Read the extract opposite from Charles Dickens's *Oliver Twist*. Oliver has run away to London, but is homeless and exhausted, when Jack Dawkins comes across him.

"Hullo, my **covey**! What's the row?"

The boy who addressed this inquiry to the young **wayfarer**, was about his own age: but one of the queerest looking boys that Oliver had ever seen. He was a snub-nosed, flat-browed, common-faced boy enough; and as dirty a **juvenile** as one would wish to see; but he had about him all the airs and manners of a man. He was short of his age: with rather bowlegs, and little, sharp, ugly eyes. His hat was stuck on the top of his head so lightly, that it threatened to fall off every moment – and would have done so, very often, if the wearer had not had a knack of every now and then giving his head a sudden twitch, which brought it back to its old place again. He wore a man's coat, which reached nearly to his heels. He had turned the cuffs back, half-way up his arm, to get his hands out of the sleeves: apparently with the ultimate view of thrusting them into the pockets of his corduroy trousers; for there he kept them. He was, altogether, as **roystering** and swaggering a young gentleman as ever stood four feet six, or something less, in his **bluchers**.

covey mate
wayfarer traveller
juvenile young person

roystering boisterous
bluchers casual shoes

1. Write a short paragraph explaining how Terry Pratchett has drawn on Dickens's original character in his own version of 'Dodger'. Think about the following:
   - Dodger's appearance
   - his attitude to others
   - his confidence and sense of self.

2. In *Dodger*, the character Charlie often jots down ideas in his notebook. He mentions phrases that will become titles of three of Charles Dickens's most famous novels: *Great Expectations, Our Mutual Friend* and *Bleak House*.

The great themes of these novels include:

- wealth and poverty
- triumph of good over evil
- love and friendship
- the river Thames
- generosity and cruelty
- a young man growing into adulthood.

How does Terry Pratchett weave these themes into *Dodger*? Write down your ideas and be prepared to share them with a partner or the whole class.

ASSESSMENT

- **Self-assessment.** Rate yourself from 1 to 3 (with 3 being the highest) on how well you compared the two Dodger characters in terms of:
  - appearance
  - attitude to others
  - confidence and sense of self.

- **Teacher assessment.** Ask your teacher to assess how well you identified and explained the key themes in *Dodger*. Ask what he or she thought were the strongest elements of your writing and which areas could do with some improvement.

3. TRACING THE PLOT

> ### Objectives
> - Consider the plot and structure of the playscript.
> - Sequence events to understand cause and effect.

Terry Pratchett echoes the structure of a classic novel by Charles Dickens in that it is made up of a sequence of dramatic episodes, full of mini-climaxes, mystery and suspense. This structure echoes the way that many of Dickens's novels were structured, published as they were as weekly episodes in magazines.

1. The playscript travels with its hero, Dodger, from the sewers to Buckingham Palace. Sort the episodes below and on page 106 into the correct order, as if in preparation for a weekly publication. There are ten episodes in total. The first one is labelled 1.

1 Dodger rescues a young lady who is fleeing from two violent men. Two gentlemen approach and offer the girl refuge. One of the men, Charlie, asks Dodger to find out who was pursuing the girl.

Dodger realizes that he and Simplicity are being hunted down. Solomon suggests that 'No one hunts a dead man'. They are invited to a social evening at Angela's where Dodger offers to take a group on a tour of London's sewers.

Simplicity tells Dodger that she is afraid of being sent back to her cruel husband. Dodger realizes that they are being followed and warns off his tracker.

On the tour, Dodger is attacked by the infamous assassin 'the Outlander'. Simplicity comes to Dodger's rescue, and then hides while Dodger borrows a corpse and pretends that Simplicity has been killed. Dodger mourns in public.

A German prince discusses the need to dispose of 'Simplicity' with a violent criminal, Sharp Bob.

Dodger returns home to Solomon, who advises him to get some better clothes from the pawn shop. He puts word out on the street for information about the attack.

Dodger goes to a barber, Sweeney Todd, to get smartened up, but Todd behaves strangely, disturbed by his war experiences. Dodger persuades Todd to hand over his cut-throat razor peacefully before the police arrive to arrest Todd. Dodger is celebrated as a hero.

Dodger visits Charlie at Fleet Street and apparently saves the offices from a villainous attacker. He begins to form an attachment to Simplicity, as she recovers.

Dodger is invited to the Palace, along with his new fiancée, Serendipity. He is knighted and accepts the offer of a job as a spy.

Dodger and Simplicity meet Charlie and Disraeli at the Houses of Parliament. Disraeli says that if Simplicity doesn't return to Germany, there will be severe consequences between the nations. Simplicity stays with Angela Burdett-Coutts for safety.

2. If you were publishing the story for the first time, what other titles might you consider? In pairs, or small groups, think up two possible titles, giving reasons for your choice. Share them with the class and vote for the most popular title.

ASSESSMENT

- **Self-assessment.** Use the playscript to check that you have sequenced the plot correctly. If you have given some of the episodes out of sequence, decide whether this order of events would affect the logic of the story.

- **Peer assessment.** Vote for the three most popular alternative titles for *Dodger*. Be prepared to explain your preferences, saying why you think some of the titles are stronger than others.

4. WHAT IS THE TRUTH?

> **Objectives**
> - Consider differences in style between journalism and diary writing.
> - Write a newspaper article reporting the arrest of Sweeney Todd and also a diary entry, recounting the same event.

In the playscript, Dickens tells Dodger that he underestimates 'the power of the press'. For stopping Sweeney Todd's seventh murder, the 'grateful Londoners' donate 50 sovereigns to Dodger, who they regard as a hero.

Dodger feels that he doesn't deserve this heroic status, as it's not quite founded on the truth of what happened. However, Dickens explains that 'the truth, rather than being a simple thing, is constructed. We journalists have to distil the truth into stories that people can understand [...] The truth is a fog, in which one man sees one thing and the other sees something totally different.'

1. With a partner, take on the roles of Dodger and Dickens. Repeat the conversation above, but in your own words. Remember that Dodger knows exactly what happened and why, but Dickens knows how journalism can give a particular viewpoint that people like to read about.

2. Plan to write two accounts of what happened at Sweeney Todd's barber shop: one for a newspaper article; the other for a diary entry written by Dodger (assuming that his writing skills were better than he admits in the playscript). You could write both with a partner or each take one task.

For each piece of writing think carefully about:
- who it is written for
- the purpose of the writing
- whether it should be told in the third person or first person
- whether to include quotations from other people
- what kind of writing style is most appropriate – colloquial, informal or in Standard English? Should it be personal, sensationalist, emotive, and/or thoughtful?

Use notes or a spider diagram like the one started below to plan your work.

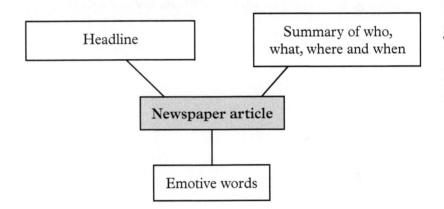

3. When you have written a first draft, swap it with your partner. Check your partner's work, proofreading it for spelling, grammar and punctuation. Comment on one aspect that you think is particularly good and another that may need a little more work.

4. Write and display your final versions.

Assessment

- **Peer assessment.** Ask another pair to comment on your work. Ask them to give you a rating from 1 to 5 (with 5 being the highest) on the aspects listed below.
  - How strongly does the newspaper article depict Dodger as a hero?
  - How thoughtfully does the diary extract show Dodger's real feelings about the events?

- **Teacher assessment.** Ask your teacher to choose the best example of a newspaper article and to explain what makes it the strongest. Then ask him or her to choose the best example of a diary extract and to explain why they think it is the most effective.

5.   AN ALTERNATIVE SCENE

Objectives

- Explore characters, their feelings and motivations through role-play.
- Improvise an alternative scene.

If Mister Sharp Bob had been successful in kidnapping Simplicity from Angela Burdett-Coutts's house, he would have taken her to the prince and the ambassador at the German Embassy. How might Dodger have reacted?

1.   In small groups, improvise a possible scene at the German Embassy. Decide who will take on the roles of:
- the German prince
- Sharp Bob
- Simplicity
- Dodger.

Additional characters could include:
- the German ambassador
- Peelers (policemen)
- the Outlander.

Before you start the improvisation, think carefully about what you have learned about your character from the playscript. Ask yourself these questions (continued on page 112):

How would my body language (e.g. expressions, gestures) reflect my feelings?

What are my strengths or source of power?

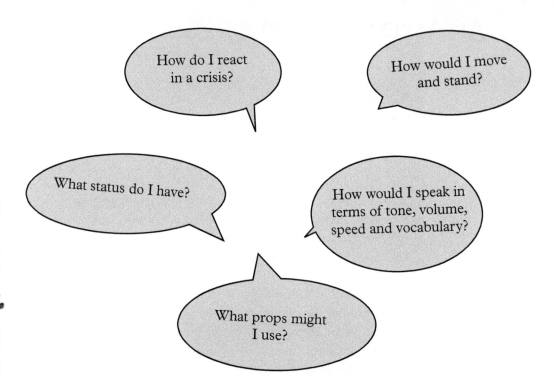

How do I react in a crisis?

How would I move and stand?

What status do I have?

How would I speak in terms of tone, volume, speed and vocabulary?

What props might I use?

2. As a group, have a brief discussion to decide on what might take place in the scene. Agree a broad outline of events, but leave the detail and wording to develop during the performance. Think about:
   - how Dodger might get into the Embassy
   - how Sharp Bob might prove himself less than 'sharp' in a crisis
   - how Simplicity might work with Dodger so they both escape
   - whether there will be violence or a fight
   - what might happen to the royal ring.

3. Perform your scene in front of another group or the class. Invite your teacher to clap when he or she wants you to 'freeze' the action. Another student should then come and tap each character on the shoulder and they have to say what they are thinking at that precise moment (in role).

4. Continue the performance until the end of the scene.

ASSESSMENT

- **Self-assessment.** Think about your personal performance. Give yourself a thumbs up 👍 or thumbs down 👎 for the following:
  - Did you manage to remain in role throughout the scene?
  - Could you describe the feelings of your character when the action froze?
  - Did you understand your character better by taking on their role?

- **Peer assessment.** Ask the rest of the group to rank in order how well you did the following (with the best first):
  - contributed to the group discussion, listening to others and offering your own ideas
  - acted your character in the scene
  - interacted with the other characters in the scene.

6. SWEENEY TODD: VILLAIN OR VICTIM?

> **Objectives**
> - Explore the moral issues surrounding crime and punishment.
> - Participate in a debate about whether Sweeney Todd should be punished or cared for.

In the playscript (and novel) Dickens persuades Dodger to accept the public money donated for his 'heroism' in disarming Sweeney Todd by suggesting that he might use it to secure Todd's future care in Bedlam Hospital. Dodger feels compassion for Todd, realizing that he has been psychologically scarred by his wartime experiences.

In the novel, Terry Pratchett adds a bonus scene at the end, in which Dodger pays Todd a visit in Bedlam Hospital. He says to Todd, 'Sometimes I feels there are no heroes, no villains. Just men, ordinary men locked up by circumstances, good or bad.' Dodger sees how the warders play along with Todd's wartime stories, to keep him calm and to focus on the good that he did.

Terry Pratchett uses this scene to highlight the debate about the care of criminals. Prepare to hold a debate about this issue, starting with Sweeney Todd's situation, but widening out into the broader topic. Follow the steps below.

Step 1
Split into two groups: those in favour of punishing all criminals; and those who feel they need care rather than punishment.

Step 2
Appoint an impartial chairperson, who will have authority to say who can speak when.

Step 3
Each group should appoint a spokesperson to represent their views.

Step 4

Each group needs to research and discuss their viewpoint and draw up a list of arguments to support it. They should also try to anticipate what their opponents might say and think of counter-arguments. Some areas to explore are shown in the boxes below. Each group should ensure that:

- Everyone has an opportunity to express his or her ideas.
- Everyone listens to what is said and responds to it.

In favour of punishing criminals
- Does punishment deter others from committing crimes?
- Do victims need to see criminals punished?
- Could all criminals claim to be mentally unstable?
- Does punishment deter criminals from further crime?

In favour of caring for criminals
- How effective is rehabilitation?
- Can crimes be seen as 'mistakes'?
- If you are mentally unwell, should you be held responsible for your actions?
- Is it fair to punish someone who is already suffering and unstable?

Step 5

Each spokesperson presents his or her group's viewpoint. He or she might find it useful to have notes to refer to during the presentation.

Step 6

The chairperson 'opens the floor' to other viewpoints – letting everyone have their say.

Step 7
A vote is taken. The side with the most votes wins.

Assessment

- **Self-assessment.** Consider how well you worked in the group. Did you:
  - listen carefully to what others said?
  - respond to what others said?
  - present your own views effectively?

- **Teacher assessment.** Invite your teacher to name two people who contributed to the discussion effectively and to comment on why their contributions were successful.

7. DEFENDING YOUR CHARACTER

> **Objectives**
>
> - Identify relevant information in the play to back up an argument.
> - In role, justify why your character is important in the play.

Sometimes directors of plays or films suggest that authors make changes to their stories in order to improve the play or film for the audience. For example, they might suggest that the author simplifies the plot, adds another twist to the plot, emphasizes a theme or reduces the number of characters.

If the director of a production of *Dodger* wanted to cut down the number of main characters in the play by one, which one would you suggest should be lost? In groups, imagine you are actors who are playing the following characters:

- Solomon
- Charles Dickens
- Dodger
- the German prince
- Simplicity
- Queen Victoria.

Write down the character names on separate pieces of paper, fold the pieces of paper and put them in a hat or small box. Ask each person to take a piece of paper to identify the role that he or she will defend.

Now imagine that the director has asked you to take turns to justify your character, explaining why you think he or she is important in the play. You will be competing to keep your job, so you must think carefully about your argument, making sure you put forward a clear case.

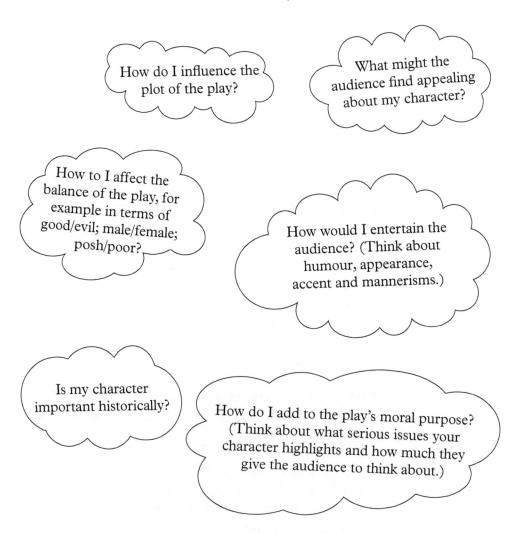

1. Spend time thinking carefully about why your character is valuable in the play. Skim and scan through the play to remind yourself of what your character says and does.

2. Ask yourself the following questions and write your answers as notes that you can refer to later.

How do I influence the plot of the play?

What might the audience find appealing about my character?

How to I affect the balance of the play, for example in terms of good/evil; male/female; posh/poor?

How would I entertain the audience? (Think about humour, appearance, accent and mannerisms.)

Is my character important historically?

How do I add to the play's moral purpose? (Think about what serious issues your character highlights and how much they give the audience to think about.)

3. Add any more information about your character that you think helps to justify keeping him or her in the play.

4. Take turns to speak up for your character. You might want to do this in the role of your character, to make a greater impact on the director. Make your arguments as persuasive as possible. You could use some of the sentence starters below to help you:

I am important to the plot of the play because...

When the audience look at me, they will feel...

I represent a serious message in the play because...

I will entertain the audience because...

ASSESSMENT

- **Self-assessment.** Think about your argument. Give yourself a thumbs up 👍 or thumbs down 👎 for how well you:
  - understood your role in the plot
  - scanned the play for relevant information
  - made notes that helped you justify your character.

- **Peer assessment.** Either select or take a vote on which character you feel should be cut from the playscript. Explain your reasons carefully, based on the arguments that were put forward by the 'actors'.

Further Activities

1. Record a short video on a mobile phone that serves to explain what *Dodger* is about and why people should watch the play or read the novel.

2. Research more about Henry Mayhew's *London Labour and the London Poor*. If a TV documentary were being made about it and you were asked to select the images and soundtrack for the opening, what would you use?

3. Role-play a meeting between Simplicity and the Outlander. Think carefully about what they might have in common, as well as how they might differ.

4. Plan a gaming app based on the character of Dodger. It could relate to his life as a 'tosher', collecting other people's lost treasures, for example. Think about sound effects, music, and skill challenges, as well as the visuals. Remember to keep your target player in mind.

5. If you were to write a novel about what is wrong with society today, what aspect would you focus on? Think of a character who might tell the story, showing the reader a particular viewpoint. Decide on a suitable title for your novel and the outline of a plot.

6. Imagine that you are Solomon and that you have been asked to write a magazine feature called 'My Life, My Views'. Draft a feature, elaborating on some of the information given in the playscript.

7. Go to Terry Pratchett's website and choose one of his novels to read and review for an online bookseller. (You might want to consider *The Amazing Maurice and his Educated Rodents* or *Johnny and the Dead*.)